FOR CORINNE.

THIS BOOK/SLIK WOULD NOT
EXIST WITHOUT YOU.

LOVE YOU TO THE MOON.

How To Read A Wine Label

Marie Cheslik

Published by Peridot Publishing

ISBN: 979-8-9999477-0-3

First Edition, 2025

How To Read A Wine Label

Marie Cheslik

CONTENTS

INTRO:

As Ruth from Ozark would say, I didn't know "shit about fuck" when it came to wine.

I was not born into some legacy winemaking family. Instead, I was born in Milwaukee, Wisconsin, where the culture embraces drinking Pabst Blue Ribbon in dive bars over fancy Michelin-starred wine lists. I left for Chicago in 2010 to pursue my Bachelor of Science in Nursing. I worked in restaurants while studying for my nursing boards exam, and saw the parallels of both hospitals and hospitality. Both careers involve chaos, camaraderie, and the constant filling of water glasses, all with the baseline desire to help people. Both fields taught me something: being a nurse showed me the importance of death and working in wine taught me the importance of life. Both are significant, but it was way more fun to talk about food, wine, and the people who make it happen, as opposed to talking about diabetes and heart failure. I quit the nursing gig and committed myself full time to the world of restaurants.

Like most people, wine was always a bit of a question mark for me. And that question mark led to more question marks, and ultimately the start of a lifelong journey. A journey that led to learning about places I didn't know existed, the multitude of climates that grapes can thrive in, the passion of the winemakers, and the challenge of describing how a wine tastes. You start to learn about the history, places, and people, which leads to clues and cues from a wine. It starts as a jumbled mess of words with no real association. You may become frustrated that you don't speak French, or you don't know if Cahors is some obscure grape varietal or a place in The Lord of the Rings. It was reminiscent of learning about health sciences, being overwhelmed by biliary duct systems and symptoms of Digoxin poisoning that you can't make sense of it all. Then one day, it does make sense and you realize that all this knowledge and practice is paying off. You get the hang of recognizing regions, grapes, and climates, you start to hone in on what you love and can articulate why you love it. You look at a wine label and realize you've had your "a-ha" moment to say, "I know these words and I'm probably gonna like this wine." You wake up one day and realize you ARE more confident. This is how we learn. This is what got me hooked.

I ignorantly dove headfirst into wine and worked at a restaurant with an extensive list of Middle Eastern wines (a traditional place to start!!). We were expected to know grape varietals, winegrowing regions, classic blends, flagship producers, and have a bedtime story for each bottle on the list. Every Wednesday, predictably called "Wine Wednesday", one of the managers would quiz us before the restaurant opened for service.

"OKAY, MARIE (he had a habit of talking like this), what are the classic blending grapes for a Left Bank Bordeaux?"

White knuckling the restaurant wine list, I hoped that the answer would come to me via osmosis (it didn't). I started stage one of the grieving process: denial. Why was I expected

How To Read A Wine Label

to know this if the average diner didn't and frankly didn't care? I skipped stages two, three, and four of the grieving process and catapulted into the final phase: acceptance.

"Well, I guess I'm a big stupid idiot," I conceded. No one laughed.

One pulverized ego later, I made sure that moment didn't happen again. At a minimum, being able to learn more about wine would not only save me from pre-shift degradation, but would add a valuable asset to my hospitality toolbelt. Aside from the fear of public humiliation, there is an undeniable factor of economics that plays into wine knowledge. As a server or sommelier, if you sold a $500 bottle of wine, you'd likely get a bigger tip (#math). That same manager put a new $900 wine on the list and started a competition where whoever sold it would get an extra $100. That was enough motivation for the minimum-wage, Taco Bell-loving ($100 bucks is like, what, 20 Crunchwraps?) service team to attempt a tableside pitch for the wine. After some aggressive Googling, there wasn't much information aside from the fact that it was from the Upper Galilee mountains and the wine was called "Enigma". That night, we took our chances selling the bottle at every table where the diners were wearing designer clothes. We had one VIP table that night in Natasha's section. Now Natasha was a killer salesperson with a killer personality. If anyone was selling this wine, it was her.

We tried to get in earshot of her sales pitch, but there was a lot of laughing, smiling, slight arm grazing, and did I even see her wink? Damn, she's good... am I in love? She sold the bottle.

Her secret? Years of on-the-spot comedy improv trained her for moments like this.

"I told them that the wine was supposed to be a horrible vintage that year, but it ended up being extraordinary. Hence the name 'Enigma'," she purred with satisfaction. She knew she couldn't even get in trouble because her on-the-spot lie was that clever.

Now, making up a story about the name of the wine? Not recommended. Getting the $100 and buying a round of beers for the staff that night? Admirable. I am not saying it's okay to lie, but I am saying that there's plenty to discern from simply looking at a label. This sparked something in me – if the guest is going to pick a bottle and stare at the label with me while I present it tableside, I should be able to talk about the visual points on the label. Why is it called 'Enigma'? Why is there an illustration of a guy who looks like the neighborhood milkman? Can you point to the Upper Galilee mountains on a map? Instead of signing up for improv classes, I took the seemingly easier route of hitting the books. I buckled down and started studying.

I passed the Certified Sommelier Examination within the Court of Master Sommeliers and worked my way up from server to wine director at a Michelin-starred restaurant in Chicago. I came in early to taste wines, made flashcards, and traded snacks from the kitchen in exchange for a sizable sip of baller wine. During this time, I received a piece of serendipitous advice from a colleague: "The fastest way to learn about wine is by reading and understanding every word on the label." Yet another hint from the universe about the importance of knowing a wine label. I used this nugget of knowledge to become a better salesperson, storyteller, and sommelier. I spent that time curating the wine list, collaborating with the chefs to create wine pairings for the tasting menu, and teaching the staff to find their way around a wine label through a "show and tell" exercise. Servers would pick a bottle they were interested in from the list and show it off to the group. They broke down each word on the label, explained what it would pair well with from the menu, and gave their best tableside spiel. I was nominated for Best Sommelier in the Jean Banchet Awards and for an Eater's Young Guns award the year I took over the program.

Cue March 16, 2020, and my restaurant career came to a halt; I was thankful for those nursing continuing education credits I took while juggling life as a wine director. I worked as a travel nurse during Covid, paid off my student loans, and started Slik Wines to teach people about wine and connect with them in a safe, virtual environment. Educating lawyers, stay-at-home parents, consultants, doctors, teachers, business analysts, and even other nurses about wine was no different than teaching staff in a restaurant. I made short videos on the internet to get everyday folk excited about wine and prove that it was more approachable than people give it credit for.

Taking feedback from my classes and videos, I asked attendees what they thought was the most intimidating aspect about wine. The majority said they never felt confident choosing a wine in a store and would joke that they picked a wine "because [they] liked the label." This full-circle moment finally permeated my thick skull. Understanding wine labels was a recurring theme that I didn't, and frankly still don't, see sommeliers explaining in plain English to everyday people. All those aspects to a wine label are context clues that not only help professionals but everyday wine drinkers.

I'm a believer in teaching someone how to fish (creating a book on how to read wine labels) rather than just giving them a fish (telling you what to drink). Let's make one thing clear: if some ding-dong Midwesterner like myself can figure out this whole wine thing, I know you can too.

Wine professionals will advise people to "just start drinking" if they want to know more about wine. That's not untrue, but it's also not helpful. The next logical question would be, "What should I drink and why?" I want you to feel that same sense of satisfaction that I did when all the pieces start coming together.

The goal of this book is to help you buy a great bottle of wine you'll like without needing to taste it. I won't quiz you on the classic blending grapes of Left Bank Bordeaux, but we will see if we can identify a Bordeaux by reading the label, what it might taste like, and most importantly if you might enjoy it. We will be asking not the "what" of wine, but the "why" and "how". For some, accurately reading labels might spark curiosity, bud into confidence, and then perhaps blossom into a lifelong wine journey.

HOW TO USE THIS BOOK

I'll tell you what we're not going to do: We are not going to do deep dives on specific regions, winemaking techniques, quality-level designations, or vintage charts. There are lots of resources to get nerdy, but this book is for curious consumers or aspiring wine professionals trying to find a bottle of wine that's right for them.

If it's your first time reading, I suggest reading page to page. Starting with forming personal preferences and your own vocabulary to describe a wine you like (or don't like), then moving on to core concepts, then finally getting some good practice on how to read a label. If you're a really fast reader, you can probably crush this book before the store clerk kicks you out for not buying anything. This resource will help you wet your whistle just enough to start looking at wine labels today.

Once you've read this once or twice, I'd even suggest making flashcards to help you remember these core regions, grapes, and terms. If you're really into it, start studying the specific topics you enjoy or challenging yourself by reading every wine label in the store. If you've hit that last point, I'm afraid it's too late for you. You're officially 'into wine', which is a blessing to your overall outlook on life but a curse to your bank account.

Within wine, there are many exceptions to the rules with new trends and techniques popping up every day. You might not nail it every time, but as our patron saint Anthony Bourdain says, "If you don't risk the bad meal, you'll never get the magical one." Experience is the ultimate teacher, but learning the building blocks in this book will give you the best chance of finding that magical bottle with the least amount of pain.

IF YOU HAVE A HARD TIME DESCRIBING WINE, READ THIS...

If you've recently been to a wine tasting and said that a wine, "Smells like grapes," you may want to read this section first. In this chapter, the goal is establishing a baseline of the skills you will need in order to know what a wine will taste like without opening it, and those skills will help you understand the next sections more comprehensively. If you feel a bit more confident, feel free to skip to the Building Blocks section.

LET ME ASK YOU A QUESTION: *WHAT'S IN A MARTINI?*

If you asked a bartender, you'd likely get the Classic Martini, which is gin and vermouth, stirred and strained in a Martini glass. If you asked my mother-in-law, it would be 3 ounces of ice-cold vodka and shaken so you get little bits of ice in there (it needs to be cold AF). Someone else might say it's vodka with a splash of olive juice and blue-cheese stuffed olives. Ask three people to make a Martini and you'd get three different beverages. Now, if we're being pedantic, the bartender has the "correct" version of a Martini, but the problem is that people don't want to necessarily live their life on what is "correct" but what they enjoy drinking. One person won't always smell the same things in a wine as another, or the "correct" thing to smell or taste. Forming your own taste is subjective, unless you grow up in a culture where we all objectively agree on culinary language.

In France, there's a tabletop board game called 'Le Loto des Odeurs' or 'Follow Your Nose', in which you smell plastic vials of clear liquid that contain particular scents. Some aromas include: lemon, eucalyptus, orange, fennel, mushrooms, hazelnut, and a scent vaguely described as 'cookie'. The goal of the game is to match the scents in the vials to a small notecard of 6 randomly selected scents. The first person to correctly match all the scents with the pictures wins. The game was invented by a former perfume maker with the goal of "discover[ing] our world through a new sensory dimension".

To be able to read a label and ultimately choose a wine depends on understanding what YOU like in a wine. To do that, we all need to train our noses and palates.

Our sense of smell is probably the most neglected and misunderstood of the five senses. We actively use our eyes, ears, touch, and taste every day, but smell is something we don't always think about. So, when people are put in a position to describe a wine, most beginners will freeze and, in that moment, forget everything they've ever smelled in their entire lives. We know what a cup of morning coffee smells like, but we use other visuals (brown liquid in a ceramic mug) and auditory cues (my Mr. Coffee automatically goes off at 6am) to reaffirm that it is indeed coffee we are smelling. When you stare into a glass of wine, there is nothing there to help you, only the smells and the little hamster wheel in your brain working overtime.

There is a physiological connection between smells, memories, and emotions. A part of your brain called the limbic system houses the amygdala and thalamus, which regulate emotion and store memories (plus some other important stuff like keeping your heart beating). The limbic system is located next to your olfactory system, which is your sense of smell. Studies suggest that proximity in the brain means that the anatomy share more neural pathways and therefore have a stronger relation to each other. This means your sense of smell is likely tied with your memories and emotions. I remember my grandma would make spiced pumpkin bread, and now for me the smell of cinnamon and cloves triggers a deep emotional (and hunger) cue. Freshly opened plastic bags evoke a strong memory of my list of chores as a kid and the house in Marietta, Georgia, where we lived for two years. I smell some of these things in wine from time to time, because I am hardwired to do so, but also because I practice smelling.

Learning how to smell and describe what you're smelling is like going to the gym. To start, you don't know how any of the machines work and you're intimidated by the buff guy on the StairMaster. You're not quite sure how to efficiently squat or do a pull-up, but you just start trying. After a while, you understand when to exercise what muscle, what days to do cardio, what days to rest. Identifying smells is the same thing. You start with "smells like grapes", but after a while you'll start recognizing it "smells fruity", then you'll note specific fruits like "cranberries", and then "those craisins that come in the blue-and-white bag at the grocery store." When learning a new instrument, we have to learn to master the basic scales (smells like strawberries) before we start playing jazz (craisins in a plastic bag).

It's also worth mentioning that where you grew up has a significant impact on what you smell. Growing up in the American Midwest, I am more likely to pinpoint fried cheese curds, mint chip ice cream, cow manure, and a half-frozen Lake Michigan on the first cold day. If I had grown up in Vietnam, I'd be more likely to pick up fresh herbs, nuróc châm, moped exhaust, and a rice patty field on a humid summer morning. Smells are deeply personal and can mean different things to different people. So, start with the basics available to you (like this book!), then expand according to your own personal experiences and environment.

To understand a wine label, we all need to use the same vocabulary to best communicate what each wine would smell and taste like. After all, tasting is mostly smelling, and that's why you can't taste anything if your nose is stuffed up from a seasonal cold. Since we don't have a collective, cultural agreement of smells like Le Loto des Odeurs, many wine educators take creative freedoms in conveying this. Whether it's teaching about congestive heart failure or wine, I find that if you use anything above a fifth-grade reading level it is a losing battle. In this book, you'll see me using broad, simple words like "fruity", "earthy", "big", and "light". Although it's fun to wax poetic and dive into obscure tasting notes, for the sake of educating beginners I KISS (keep it simple, stupid).

Describing wines takes practice and with intention. I've created some games and strategies to help you to learn how to put a name to what you're smelling and determine what you do or don't like about a wine.

Now shut up and let's KISS.

DISCOVERING YOUR WINE PREFERENCES

WHO ARE YOU?

Have you ever sat in a room by yourself with no distractions, no telephone, no music, and really asked, "Who am I?" Why do you do what you do? (I promise this is related to wine, just stick with me.) What informs your decision-making process? Is that little voice in your head yours or does it belong to your parents? Your boss? Your spouse? A stranger? Do you pick your hobbies based on personal enjoyment or how other people may perceive you? Do you like rock climbing or do you want to be that person who rock climbs?

You want to be honest with yourself about why you drink wine and what wines you like. It is completely, 100% okay that you drink wine to look cool, to look knowledgeable, or to look rich. There are lots of resources for people who want to memorize producers and the classic, great wines, and be able to talk about them in a room of professionals. I'm here to teach you the critical thinking skills of knowing how to fish, not tell you what fish to buy. This is a book to help you know how a wine will taste without opening it, form personal preferences, and then you can decide the best wine for the situation.

Although those French kids in the last chapter may have a leg up on you, you can start building your wine preferences and expand your vocabulary today for free. There is no "right" or "wrong" to what you like, but I have some games you can play by yourself or with friends that will help you articulate those preferences.

These games are based on one concept that professional sommeliers use when assessing wine: blind tasting. Blind tasting is when you taste a wine without knowing what it is. Sommeliers trying to accomplish a certification goal, like The Court of Master Sommeliers or WSET, have a certain amount of time to determine the grape, region, and even how old a wine is. For professionals, the goal is to guess the wine correctly. For the rest of us, it's a great way to be able to objectively look at a wine and have a conversation without pretense or knowing the price or if you "should" like it. For my inner-Milwaukeean, this is basically a drinking game where you might learn something. Each of these games include a blind-tasting element, and have been used to teach thousands of people how to determine what they enjoy and, more importantly, what they don't.

Game 1: The Kitchen Sink
People Required: 1 or more
What You'll Need: A kitchen with food (if you don't have that please call a friend or your mum)

Stop what you're doing right now and go to your kitchen. Close your eyes and smell everything. Pick up whatever is in your fruit bowl. There's a good chance you have an apple. Put it to your face and tell me what you smell... have you ever thought about what an apple actually smells like? What makes the smell of an apple different from a peach or a pear? What color is the apple? Would a red apple smell different than a Honeycrisp or a bright green Granny Smith? What if that apple were baked into a pie, how would it smell?

Now let's say you have a banana. Consider the condition of the banana: Is it perfectly ripe? Underripe? Overripe? How about one that's left in your garbage for a bit too long? A green banana is a bit astringent and starchy and the nearly black banana is a bit fermented but has a deep, sweet caramel smell.

Don't forget the spice cabinet too. Randomly pick out a few spices and see if you can guess what they are just by smelling them. No cheating! You're only cheating yourself, young grasshopper. If you smell cinnamon, do you think there would be a difference between ground cinnamon and whole sticks of cinnamon? If you have both, try to see if you can guess the stick of cinnamon vs. the ground cinnamon. Do this with cardamom, allspice, cloves, fennel, and whatever else you may have. Being able to pinpoint hyperspecific tasting notes like 'Berry Berry Kix' or 'Grandpa's linen shirt after he smokes a cigar' takes practice. Start simple, then go crazy.

Game 2: Jellybean Blind Tasting
People Required: 1 or more
What You'll Need: A package of jellybeans or gummy bears

Go to the store and pick up your favorite bag of jellybeans (I'm a big fan of the Jelly Belly), but you want a candy that gives you a guide of what the flavors are on the bag. Reach into the bag and, without peeking, eat half of the jellybean and see if you can guess the

flavor using the guide on the back. It helps to have a word bank to start so you're not just guessing from everything you've ever tasted in your entire life. Once you've made your guess you can analyze the color of the uneaten jellybean. It's a fun game to play alone or with your friends if your friends are into weirdo tasting games like this.

Game 3: Pinot Noir vs Pinot Noir
People Required: 2 or more
What You'll Need: 2 bottles of wine, glassware, a tasting grid, and an optional flavor wheel

A game you can try at home is doing a classic side-by-side blind tasting. It goes like this: have an innocent third party pick two Pinot Noirs, one from France and one from the US. Cover them with a sock or brown bag, and have a friend or loved one pour them randomly for you. You won't know which Pinot Noir is which, but it'll help you understand a building-block concept: New World vs Old World. You may be surprised that even though they're the same grape, they smell different!

See if you can smell if one is more fruit forward and what that might mean. If it's more earthy or subtle, what would that mean? If you're not sure of the answer to that, the New World vs Old World section will be the one for you. You can also do a grape varietal side-by-side blind tasting.

Not sure of the differences between a Pinot Noir and Cabernet Sauvignon? How about a Cabernet Sauvignon and a Malbec? Try them blind! Blind tasting is one of my favorite ways to solidify what I have learned and pick up on the nuances that we talk about in this book. I've added my tasting grid I've used for teaching students and it's yours to keep as a nice guide!

Some people find it helpful to have a vocabulary list of smells in the form of a flavor wheel and they're trying to describe wines. I've encouraged people to make their own with common tasting notes you use or you can use Wine Folly's flavor wheel as an ol' reliable (just a Google search away).

Slik

BLIND TASTING GUIDE

WINE #

◯

SIGHT

RED	RUBY	GARNET	PURPLE

STRAW	YELLOW	GOLDEN	AMBER

CLARITY	CLEAR	HAZY	CLOUDY

NOSE

INTENSITY	LOW	MEDIUM	HIGH
FRUITS			
FLOWERS			
HERBS			
SPICES			
EARTH			
OAK			

PALATE & STRUCTURE

ACID	LOW	MEDIUM	HIGH
TANNIN	LOW	MEDIUM	HIGH
BODY	LIGHT	MEDIUM	FULL
SWEETNESS	DRY	OFF-DRY	SWEET

CONCLUSION

◯ NEW WORLD   ◯ OLD WORLD

VARIETAL	
COUNTRY	
VINTAGE	

DO YOU LIKE THIS WINE?

☹ 😕 😐 🙂 😊

◯ DON'T SEE YOUR FEELING?
DRAW YOUR OWN.

How To Read A Wine Label

BUILDING BLOCKS

The following are critical thinking exercises that help to understand why a wine has a specific flavor profile or style. If I was teaching you as a beginner sommelier in my restaurant, this is what you would learn. Imagine these chapters as building out your wine skeleton and, as you progress, you'll add muscles, neurons, and even a lymphatic system if you're feeling wild.

Think of these building blocks as a framework, not a rule book. Distinctions are helpful, but they are not absolute, and you'll quickly find exceptions to the rules and technicalities. Most wine professionals will point out these exceptions from the jump. I won't mince words: I hate these people. Pointing out minute differences hinders the sake of progression as a whole and is not helpful when you're first starting.

It reminds me of new doctors showing off their knowledge to their first patients. They worked hard to get there, they certainly know more about disease processes than I do (but not as much as the Filipino charge nurse) but knowing something is entirely different than knowing when to apply it (knowledge vs wisdom, as they say). For example, say you're a doctor explaining a new diabetes medication called metformin to your patient. You could tell your patient, "This medication activates AMP-activated protein kinase by inhibiting the mitochondrial respiratory chain, which leads to decreased production of glucose and increased insulin sensitivity in the liver and muscle tissue." However, their eyes would glaze over, just like yours might have during that last sentence. The patient might nod and go "uh-huh, okay," but as professionals we need to have a better understanding of when people, well, understand things. It would be more effective to say, "I'm putting you on a new diabetes medication and it is mostly processed through the liver and kidneys. It would be best if you quit drinking, and we'll track your bloodwork." Are you doing a disservice by excluding the part about how muscles are also affected or not letting them know more details about how the medication works? No. Talk about the contraindications and comorbidities with the cardiologist and Dr. McDreamy. Leave the day-to-day activities and practical next steps for your patient living with it.

Now replace "doctors" with "wine professionals". Learning about winemaking techniques, clones of varietals, and soil types is incredibly interesting and helpful for a select few. If you were to bring up the state-of-the-art Cryo-Maceration that Bending Branch Winery in Texas is pioneering with their Tannats, most people might nod their head and say "uh-huh, okay." Is it important and really cool? Totally, yes. Do people who are choosing wine at a grocery store care about that? Likely not.

A wine label is a story told in fragments. Some parts are required by law to be there, and some are creative freedoms that the winemaker takes. To read one is to sift through layers of bureaucracy, tradition, and a bit of marketing. The trick isn't memorization; it's learning which details matter and which exist to charm your dinner party guests.

Consider the mandatory elements first those dull but essential declarations required by governments and wine regulators. These form the backbone of any label, the parts that winemakers can't fudge without risking fines or worse. The region, for instance, isn't just geography: it's a set of rules. A bottle labeled "Barolo" isn't merely from Piedmont; it's made from Nebbiolo, aged for a certain amount of time, and held to standards that their geographic neighbors escapes. The alcohol percentage, too, is more revealing than it seems. A German Riesling at 8% ABV will be a different beast than one at 13%, and not just in strength but in flavor. The former practically guarantees a sweeter wine, while the latter suggests a drier, more structured wine.

Then there's the winemaker's own narrative the flourishes and embellishments that transform a government-mandated fact sheet into something resembling art. A family crest might signal generations of tradition, or it might be a clever bit of branding dreamed up at the last board meeting. A name like "Ruff Day" with a dog on the label tells you nothing about what's in the bottle but everything about the people behind it. These details are where personality seeps in, where you get a glimpse of whether the producer sees themselves as a steward of terroir or silly goober who wants to have a fun time.

The hierarchy of text alone can be revealing. When "Sancerre" appears in larger type than the winery's name, it's a statement: this wine is about place first, producer second. The absence of a grape variety on a French bottle isn't an oversight; it's a quiet insistence that soil matters more than varietal. Even the style of the font can hint at priorities. A minimalist label with intriguing lettering suggests a different audience than a bottle adorned with a gilded coat of arms.

Learning to decode all this isn't about studying flashcards, it's about training yourself to ask the right questions and notice the right things. These building blocks of understanding climate, geography, and cultural influences will get you to the gooey center of what's practical when reading a wine label. By proxy, you will also learn the critical thinking skills to assess labels from wine regions not included in this book. The answers aren't always consistent, but the act of questioning is what turns a casual drinker into someone who truly understands what they're holding.

Next time you pick up a bottle, don't just glance at it. Break it down to what you know what you don't. The label knows more than it's telling you. Your job is to make it talk (and maybe look a few things up).

OLD WORLD VS NEW WORLD

The first of the core concepts is Old World vs New World. Understanding this will help you recognize how a region's culture, history, and geography can ultimately decide the style and taste of a wine.

When we say the Old World, we're talking about European wine-producing countries. Think France, Italy, Spain, Germany, Greece, and the like. The Old World wasn't the first region to make wine (the republic of Georgia would be the first to take that title), but it was the first to define

How To Read A Wine Label

quality standards and market it globally. The French get the most credit for creating classification systems for wines, ensuring that they preserve the quality and identity of a wine from a region. You'll learn more about this in the next chapter, Here's the Thing About Europe. Italy and France are the proudest when it comes to the consistency that each region brings, hence you'll see that reflected more on the label. The French even coined the word "terrior" to encompass the physical and cultural factors of wines grown in a region. Essentially: terrior = vibes. Wines from the Old World are generally more subtle, meaning you'll likely have to really stick your nose in the glass to smell something, and usually taste earthy components like potting soil, dirt, rocks, salt, or tart fruits like cranberries, raspberries, and lemons.

The New World is not European wine-making countries. Think the USA, Argentina, Chile, South Africa, New Zealand, and Australia. Anywhere that isn't Europe is considered the New World. Many New World regions have warmer weather than their Old World counterparts. This means grapes ripen more fully, producing wines with bigger, riper fruit flavors. Wines from the New World are generally louder or more expressive in the glass, meaning the smells slap you in the face without much effort. They are more likely to find the usage of new oak in classic New World wines. Oak gives the flavor of buttered popcorn or vanilla. New World winemakers often focus on the grape itself, labeling their wines by the grape used rather than by region. There's also a difference in approach: they may have learned from Old World regions but put their own spin on things.

The modern globalization of winemaking has blurred the lines between Old and New World styles. Some New World producers strive to make terroir-driven wines, mimicking Old World techniques and restraint. Meanwhile, certain Old World winemakers have embraced modern innovations, crafting wines that are riper and more accessible than their traditional counterparts. There are also questions about regions that don't traditionally fall into these categories: what about Mexico, Lebanon, or Sweden? There is a push to label wines from the Middle East as coming from the Ancient World, but it's generally not well adopted nor is there a specific style that defines the flavor. Professionals acknowledge there's room for change, but I'll be talking about the binary when talking about reading a wine label.

There's also the matter of climate change. Regions that were once considered cool climate, like Burgundy or Northern Italy, are seeing warmer growing seasons, resulting in wines with riper fruit flavors. Conversely, some warmer climate New World producers are planting vineyards in cooler, higher-altitude areas to create fresher, more balanced wines. These shifts challenge the traditional categories and remind us that wine is a living, evolving thing.

Here is a helpful map of typical New World and Old World wine regions:

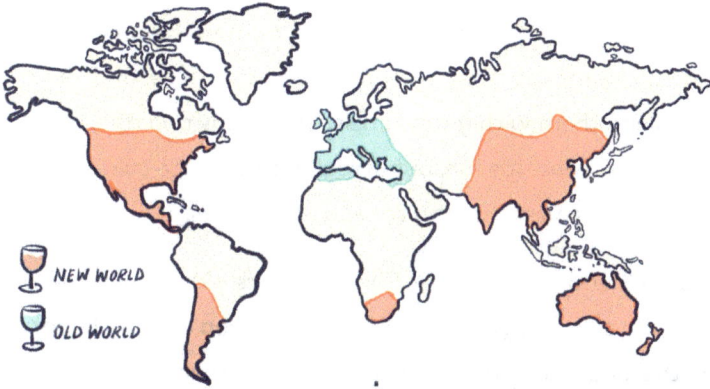

NEW WORLD

OLD WORLD

OLD WORLD
- EUROPE
- SUBTLE
- TART FRUITY/EARTHY
- TRADITION
- EMPHASIS ON REGION

NEW WORLD
- NOT EUROPE
- LOUD
- JUICY FRUIT/OAKY
- INNOVATION
- EMPHASIS ON VARIETAL

HERE'S THE THING ABOUT EUROPE...

Many winemakers today understand the importance of an eye-catching label. Don't get me wrong, part of me loves this, but having a kitten playing a keytar on the label doesn't really tell me how the wine will taste. There are established wineries that don't really care about changing the label because they're an established brand/house. Some winemakers can do this because they already know the rules and enjoy breaking them with goofy labels. In this day and age, goofy labels sell wine. It's fun, but in reality this can be challenging when you're first learning to read wine labels.

For better or worse, most Europeans are old school when it comes to wine regulation. They have a proud culinary history with world-class products that they believe need government protection for quality assurance. In fact, they set up entire certification systems around it.

To fully understand this, I'll tell you a story I call the Prosciutto Parable.

You can buy prosciutto, a cured ham product, from just about anywhere. Even though it is Italian in origin, you can make cured ham in Milwaukee, Wisconsin, and still call it prosciutto if it's made from the right part of the pig. Italians see this and go, "That American crap isn't as good as ours." This was the inspiration for creating rules in the EU that protect the namesake of a regional food product. You can make prosciutto anywhere, but you can only make prosciutto di Parma (di = from, Parma = an Italian town) from the fabulous town of

Parma located in Puglia, Italy. In Parma, they feed the pigs a luxurious diet of whey and local foliage, and enforce a longer cure time for the meat. This indicates a higher level of yumminess and scrutiny before it hits the global marketplace. So, the Italians believe they have a better prosciutto than Milwaukee and made the label to say so. I'll leave it to the Italians and Italian-Americans to duke that one out.

The concept seeps into wine culture, too. Sure, you can grow Sauvignon Blanc in France, but depending on where you grow it you may see a term on the label that reads Vin de France (literally meaning Wine of France) or Sancerre (a specific place in France). As we learned from the Prosciutto Parable, indicating a specific region enforces a higher standard and consistency of taste.

If you should take anything from this book: in general, European wine is labeled by region, and wines made anywhere else are labeled by grape.

When I started working in wine, this drove me bananas. Americans are not only supposed to memorize these new places with unfamiliar names but also the grapes associated with them. In reality, the average European doesn't even know the grapes used in Chablis. They will simply ask for, "a Chablis," or they'll tell their friends, "I love a Rioja". So don't get too caught up in that nitty gritty for now. Understanding this core concept will make European wines easier to decipher.

WARM CLIMATE VS COOL CLIMATE

Wine is plants. Plants that ultimately depend on the climate of a region to achieve the wine's final result. The best way to show the climate's effect on how a wine will taste is through my tomato analogy. Imagine a tomato growing on a vine in peak summer: sweet, deep red, and juicier than the Juicy Couture jumpsuit you had in high school. This is what BLT dreams are made of. This is what happens to grapes in warm climates, they have the time to convert citric and malic acid into fructose, aka fruit sugar, due to the sunlight and heat. Warm climates mean you're likely to get rich, full-bodied, and fruit-forward wines that taste like blackberry jam or ripe pineapples. Warm-climate wines tend to be considered "juicy" or "rich".

Now imagine a green tomato on the vine: these tomatoes are physiologically mature but have not converted all the acids into sugars like those red tomatoes. You're left with a mouth-puckering, astringent product perfect for frying, grilling, or preserving. This is what happens to grapes in cool climates, they have a harder time ripening, which leaves you with light-bodied, tart fruit- forward flavors like lemons or underripe berries. These mouth-watering wines that are usually considered "fresh" or "zippy". Due to the higher acid levels, cool-climate wines tend to be more food friendly. Imagine these wines as like spritzing a zesty lemon onto a dish.

THE TOMATO ANALOGY

RED TOMATO	GREEN TOMATO
↓	↓
WARM CLIMATES	COOL CLIMATES
• FULLER-BODIED	• LIGHTER-BODIED
• JUICY FRUIT-FORWARD	• TART FRUIT-FORWARD
• RICH & JUICY	• FRESH & ZIPPY

Knowing which regions in the world are warm or cold climates will help you dictate what the wine may taste like. Ocean currents, wind currents, proximity to the equator, and altitude are some of the biggest factors in what make up the average climate of a region. There is some nuance to this. For example, you can have a warm climate like Argentina, but if you're at a higher altitude, you can produce cooler-climate results (higher altitude = colder weather. Think about how some mountains that go high enough have snow-topped peaks!). There are also Goldilocks-like temperate regions, such as Tuscany, that sit perfectly between climates, which would ultimately depend on other factors—like it being situated in the Old World—to determine flavor.

Here's a map of the general climate of regions with a quick cheat sheet of common regions you'll find on shelves.

WARM CLIMATE vs. COOL CLIMATE

CLASSIC REGIONS:

● WARM CLIMATE   ● COOL CLIMATE

THICK-SKINNED GRAPES
VS THIN-SKINNED GRAPES

The skins of wine grapes contain two major chemical compounds that will affect the color, body, and taste of a wine: tannins and pigmentation. Tannins are astringent polyphenols that contribute to structure, texture, and the aging potential of a wine. While they can create a drying sensation (think over-steeped tea, walnut skins, or green bananas), they also play a crucial role in how a wine interacts with food and develops over time. Wines with higher tannins pair better with fattier foods; in steakhouses sommeliers will jokingly call the best pairing a "Cab and a slab."

Pigmentation, specifically anthocyanins, determines a wine's color. While some research suggests anthocyanins influence mouthfeel, tannins are the primary driver of texture and perceived body. I cringe at the classic milk analogy, but it works: light-bodied wines feel like water or skim milk in the mouth; bigger-bodied wines feel more like whole milk. For the love of God, someone please contact me if you have a better analogy. I want to stop imagining drinking whole milk and wine at the same time.

Anyways, certain grape types, also called varietals, have thicker or thinner skins. If a grape has thinner skins— like Pinot Noir, for example—it has less pigmentation and tannins, leading to lighter-colored, light-bodied wines, with less tannin. Therefore, thicker-skinned grapes—like Cabernet Sauvignon—generally have more pigmentation

How To Read A Wine Label

and tannins, leading to darker- colored, bigger-bodied wines, with more tannin.

GRAPE SKINS

THIN SKINNED
(THINK GROCERY STORE GRAPES)

THICK SKINNED
(THINK CONCORD GRAPES)

When you're starting out, I suggest drinking the most classic or common grape varieties first (see the list that follows). This will give you a baseline that allows you to communicate what wines you like to the restaurant sommelier or wine shop owner. There are more than 10,000 varietals, so you're bound to run across something you're unfamiliar with, but understanding what grapes you like and why you like them will be a massive help. For example, if you like the thin-skinned, lighter-bodied, lower- tannin Sangiovese then you'll likely enjoy Grenache, Carignan, or Blaufränkisch.

Here's a cheat sheet of typical thin- and thick-skinned grapes you'll find on a label, with notable exceptions:

GRAPE SKINS: A CHEAT SHEET

	THIN SKINNED	THICK SKINNED
TRAITS	•LIGHTER COLORED WINE •LIGHTER BODIED •LESS TANNIN	•DARKER COLORED WINE •BIGGER BODIED •MORE TANNIN
WHITE GRAPES	•SAUVIGNON BLANC •PINOT GRIGIO •RIESLING	•CHARDONNAY* •MOSCATO •SEMILLON •CHENIN BLANC
RED GRAPES	•PINOT NOIR* •GAMAY •NEBBIOLO** •SANGIOVESE	•CABERNET SAUVIGNON •MERLOT •SYRAH •MALBEC •PETITE SIRAH

* It's worth nothing that these are the "chameleons" of the wine world. Both Chardonnay and Pinot Noir are enormously affected by winemaker decisions that will change the body and color of a wine. They can taste like anything, which can be annoying but also why they're intriguing. You'll want to consider the climate and region when choosing these to your liking.

** Nebbiolo is a classic exception to this rule. Even though these grapes are thin-skinned and have a lighter color, they also have some of the highest, cotton-mouth tannins out there.

ADD THIS ONCE YOU FEEL CONFIDENT

Only divulge in this section once you know the previous concepts like the back of your hand, otherwise it gets confusing!

There's a little number that features on every single bottle of wine that can give you an additional clue as to how the wine will taste. Alcohol is a byproduct of fermentation and the fuel for that process is sugar. Winemakers can influence the final alcohol level in the winemaking process, but if we use our tomato allergy, the tomato with the most sugar, aka the red tomato, aka the warm climate, will likely have a higher alcohol percentage because it has more sugars to work with. It can be helpful to know a general range of normal alcohol levels for red and white wines. This will determine if the wine is within a typical range, therefore if it's higher or lower, it can tell you a thing or two about the wine.

After much consideration of grapes, climates, winemaking, and peer review, I have decided to put these levels of alcohol into a general range. Going outside of these levels isn't necessarily bad, but it can put the wine into a more polarizing flavor profile. As you know, there are always exceptions, but use this as a guide.

TYPICAL ALCOHOL LEVELS OF WINE

RED WINES
12.5-14.5%

5%   18%

REDS < 12.5%

Very light, higher chance
of being sweet, best
served chilled.

(NEVER HAD A CHILLED RED? TRY IT SOMETIME!)

REDS > 14.5%

Big & fiery, these wines
have a higher chance of
being interpreted as
bitter, strong, or sweet.

WHITE WINES
11-14%

5%   18%

WHITES < 11%

Have a higher chance
of being a sweet wine.

WHITES > 14%

Voluptuous & coats
your mouth.

(PROFESSIONALS CALL THIS "WAXY.")

How To Read A Wine Label

Here's the giant grain of salt: US wine laws give winemakers a 1.5% leeway with their labeling. What that means is that the wine's ABV (alcohol by volume) could be 1.5% more or less than the amount on the label. EU regulations give a 0.5% leeway to winemakers. This is because wineries need to submit labels to a federal agency, whether it's the EU in Europe or the Tobacco Tax and Trade Bureau (TTB) in the US, for approval in advance to ensure the label complies with the law. These approvals take time, and the final alcohol level of a wine might not be established at the time of submission. Regardless of that caveat, I find this to be a helpful tool on our wine label journey.

SIX COMMON ITEMS ON EVERY WINE LABEL

A wine label is a map, a story, and a riddle all at once. I suggest breaking down every word on a label by reading it like a book, starting from left to right, top to bottom. Once you get the hang of it, you'll gloss over the repeatable parts, and get to the meat and potatoes of what the wine will actually taste like. The items I point out in this section will contribute to the style and quality of the wine, keeping in line with our goal of being able to know what a wine will taste like without even opening it.

Most of the repeated words/phrases you'll find on a label are government mandated. Imagine you're the boss running the ol' French wine label factory: what would be most important to you? You can feel the hot breath of the EU on your neck, so you'll want to reinforce the idea of the quality of the place, and anything that won't get you sued by someone drinking it. Everything else included is down to the creative freedom of the winery. Maybe it's a picture of their vineyard owl, or their nonna's home in the Italian countryside. These aspects are fun to dive into and make a great story when people ask you about the wine. Learning can be harder this way, but being curious about what you don't know make that information stick.

Here are six common items you'll see on every label:

1. NAME OF PRODUCER

The establishment that makes the wine. The words "winemaker", "producer", and "house" are interchangeable. In France, you'll likely see "Château," "Maison," or "Domaine" (all of which effectively mean "house"), in front of the producer's name. In Italy, you'll see "Tenuta" or "Cantina." These are usually in the biggest letters.

2. THE REGION AND ADDRESS

Where the grapes were grown and the address of the producer. You'll notice that on French wine labels, they will not list the grape varietals. Regions also have certain soil types, microclimates, and weather patterns that make each region distinct. We call the culmination of the factors "terrior", and—when you really want to be a nerd about it—you start to learn how this changes wine flavors.

3. VINTAGE

The year the grapes were harvested. Wine grapes are an agricultural product and the weather changes every year. Just like people, grapes thrive in certain weather conditions, and some grapes thrive best in certain, favorable years of perfect weather! It is up to the winemaker whether or not they present this information. Most sparkling wines sold in the US are generally blends from many vintages and will use the term "non-vintage" or NV.

4. AMOUNT OF LIQUID AND ALCOHOL PERCENTAGE

The standard size of a single bottle is 750 ml. Wines can range from around 7% ABV for a sweet wine to 18% for a wine fortified with spirits, like Port. Most dry wines today range from roughly 11.5–15%.

5. CONTAINS SULFITES

Legally this needs to be added to every wine with one part per million of sulfites. Sulfites are a preservative that naturally occurs in many products such as dried fruit, potato chips, and wine. Winemakers will add extra sulfites right before bottling to maintain the freshness of their product and create an extra safety barrier for transportation. Whether the winemaker adds extra sulfites or not, all wines meet the legal requirement to display this on their labels. Similarly to our next common item, you'll usually (not always!) find this on the back.

6. THE US GOVERNMENT WARNING

The required language enforced by federal law that states thou shalt not drink if you are pregnant or plan to drive/operate heavy machinery. You'll find this on the back label along with the importer, any certifications, and, if you're lucky, a cute little story about the winery or the wine. Because this is on the back label, we don't see too many examples in this book.

BONUS ITEMS YOU MAY FIND INCLUDE:

- The Importer, essentially the middleman between the buyer and the consumer
- Harvest Date
- Sweetness Level
- Quality Level
- Certifications for production practices such as Organic, biodynamic, Demeter, etc.
- Winery Philosophy

Part of mastery is repeating the same concepts over and over again until you know them like the back of your hand. This may feel a bit like doing math homework with your Dad late at night (and if you were like me, possibly on the verge of tears). Don't get discouraged if it doesn't click right away, these things take time and practice. You'll see similar concepts being repeated, but that is good! Once you understand these regions, you'll understand the style. Soon thereafter, you'll be able to understand how a wine may taste without even opening it! Keep that goal in mind when you're seeing these labels.

Disclaimer: No winery or importer in this book paid to be in this book. I chose these wines because they have two or three of the following: Great distribution (can be found almost anywhere), a great value for the price, is a typical example for the region and grape type. This book will focus mainly on classic regions you'd learn about in sommelier school and wines typically sold in supermarkets around the world. Perhaps there will be an "adventurous regions" book in the future, but not today (does that sound cool? Email me if that sounds cool.)

We're going to start with The USA because the New World usually contains the least amount of information and requires the least amount of context. They are the easiest of the wine labels to start with: The T-ball of the wine world. In the spirit of meeting people where they're at, we'll start with recognizable labels/producers so you have opportunities to practice in any scenario. Then we'll build up to the Major Leagues: term-ridden Old World wines plus bespoke, sommelier-favorite producers. I even threw in some Extra Credit labels in there, most of which come from lesser-known regions. Everything I will point out or elaborate on will either describe how the wine will taste, quality factors that affect the price and flavor of a wine, or unique talking points about the wine. Everything else will be things that are standard to every wine label, either legally or culturally, and are addressed earlier in the chapter. Are you ready?

Let's play ball.

USA

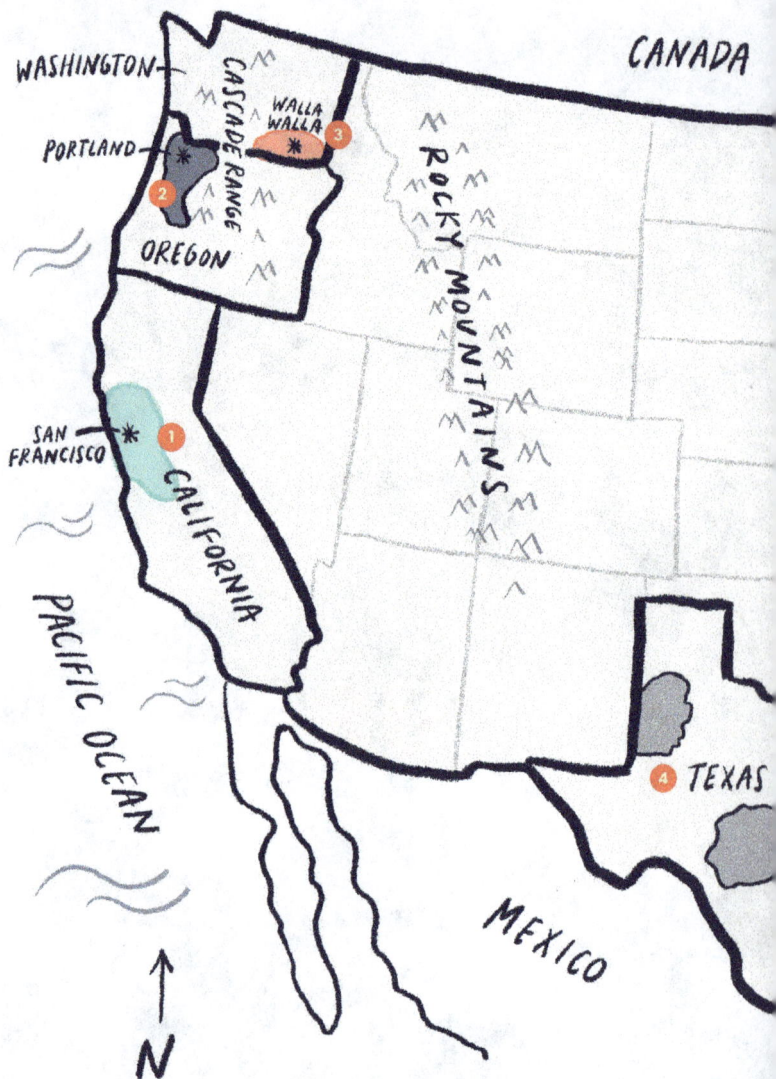

Region & Wine You'll Find:

1 **California**
Cabernet Sauvignon, Pinot Noir, Chardonnay, Merlot, Zinfandel

2 **Oregon**
Pinot Noir, Chardonnay

3 **Washington**
Syrah, Cabernet Sauvignon, Chardonnay

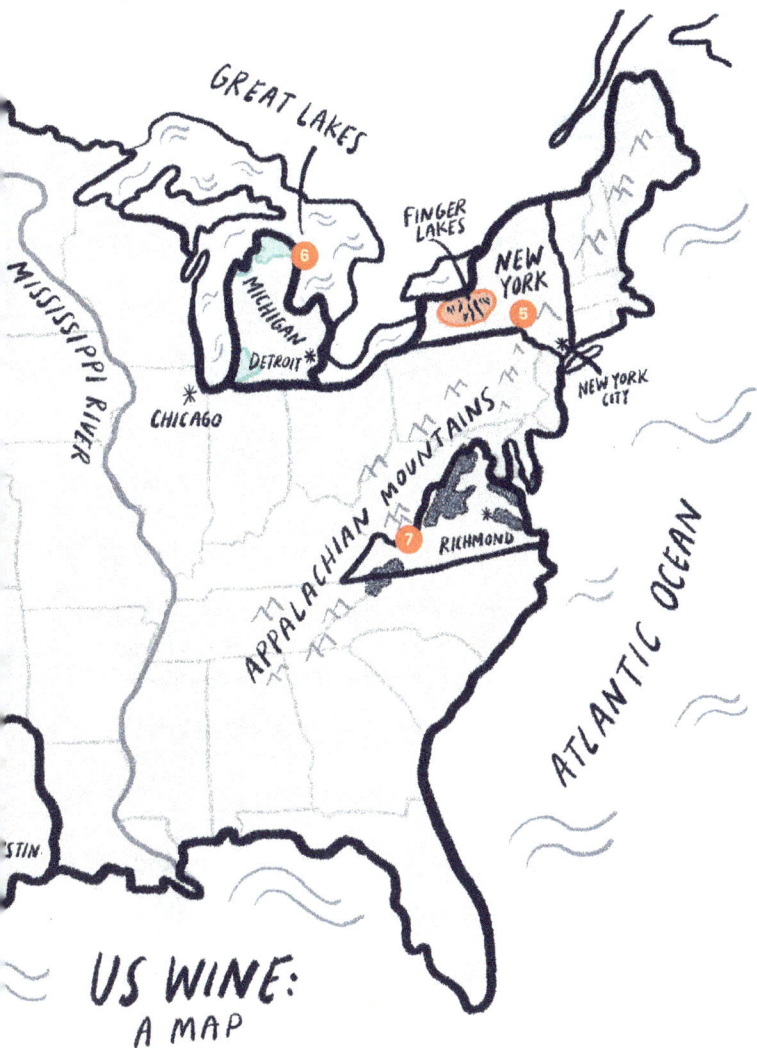

GREAT LAKES

FINGER LAKES

NEW YORK

MICHIGAN

Detroit *

CHICAGO *

MISSISSIPPI RIVER

APPALACHIAN MOUNTAINS

RICHMOND

NEW YORK CITY

ATLANTIC OCEAN

'STIN

US WINE:
A MAP

4 Texas
Tempranillo, Tennat, Cabernet Sauvignon, Vermentino

5 New York
Riesling, Cabernet Franc

6 Michigan
Riesling, Pinot Noir, Cabernet Franc

7 Virginia
Cabernet blends, Cabernet Franc, Viognier

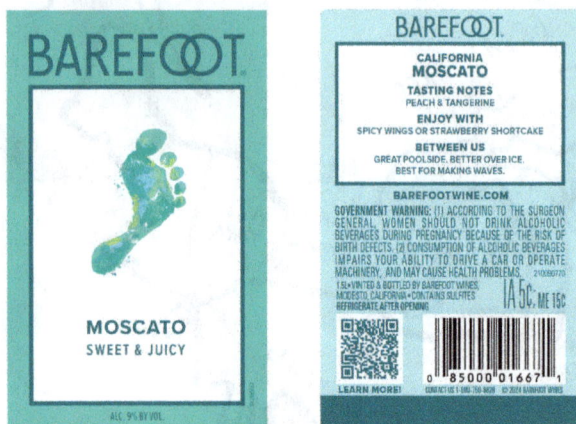

Many people, myself included, started their wine journey with a rousing game of "slap the bag" at a collegiate house party. "Game" is a loose term, but it goes like this: slap the bag of wine before you drink it out of the spigot. Although Barefoot doesn't come in adult Capri-Sun pouches (yet), it evokes the same spirit of camaraderie and accessible wine drinking. A perfect place to start our wine label journey.

Barefoot: The name of the producer or the company that makes the wine.

Moscato Sweet & Juicy: Moscato is a thick-skinned, white grape of Italian origin, which is used in this wine. Barefoot really wanted to make sure you knew what you were signing up for: a sweet wine. So they wrote it in plain English. Not every producer will give you this information explicitly. Let's play a game where we pretend they didn't tell us this was wine sweet. Do you remember which building block can help you determine whether this is sweet or not? (Keep reading for the answer.)

Alc 9% by vol: Alcohol percentage will be your biggest hint as to whether a wine is sweet or dry. As per our building block parameters, this falls firmly into the "likely sweet" category. This confirms Barefoot's claim on the front label that it's "sweet & juicy".

California Moscato: Our first regional clue! California is located in the New World, aka not Europe, which is characterized by bold, fruity flavors. So, although they are using an Old World grape like Moscato, they have taken the freedom to make the wine however they'd like.

Tasting Notes...: Something I love about New World wines is that many producers will try to make a practical blip of information for the everyday drinker. From my experience, this helps many people decide if they like a wine and what to pair it with. This information is an anomaly, unfortunately, but I'm hoping this book brings to light how useful this information can be and how more people should do it! Just remember that taste is a bit subjective, so take these notes and pairings with a grain of salt and follow your heart with your own ideas.

1.5 L: That's two 750ml bottles in one big bottle, which is called a magnum. Hell yeah.

Disclaimer: Costco has paid me zero dollars to say this but the Kirkland Selections are some of the best deals happening in America. Costco's business model goes something like this: they make all of the money on a $60-ish yearly membership then after that, they basically cover their costs with a tiny profit margin. They make money on the memberships, not the $5 rotisserie chicken or even the bottles of Kirkland Signature wine. If you're getting into wine, consider getting a Costco or other club membership and trying Kirkland Signature as a solid start to your wine journey.

Kirkland Signature: The name of the producer. Someone has the coolest job in the world to find wine or wineries that make enough to satisfy the need that they have (hint: it's a lotta hootch). They're big on quality so they will work with pretty stellar winemakers from all across the world to make the juice for their KS line. They ensure that the wines are a great representation of the region and varietal so that they can even be used for amateurs getting into wine and blind tasting. Although the names of the winemakers are sometimes disclosed on the back, it's usually under wraps to who's making the wine.

Pinot Noir: A varietal on a label! This is a big indicator we're in New World territory. This is a light-bodied red wine that acts a bit like a chameleon. These can range from bold and expressive to light and fruity, the alcohol percentage would give you a better idea of what side this Pinot Noir falls into.

Russian River Valley: A specific wine-growing region in Sonoma County, California. We've hit a deeper level of specificity, which means a higher level of quality (remember the Prosucitto Parable?)! Russian River Valley is an AVA (this is the American version of an AOC or DOC meaning 'American Viticultural Area') within Sonoma and grows mainly Pinot Noir and Chardonnay. Sonoma and RRV is technically a cooler climate region within a warm region (California) due to the early morning fog coming from the Pacific Ocean, so the wines have a nice, crisp balance to these New World wines.

Sonoma County: A wine-growing region within northern California. Napa and Sonoma usually get bunched together because they're neighbors and the Venn Diagram of varietals they use are almost a circle. When you first start out, it's more important to know that Sonoma = California = New World. As you get a bit deeper, you could even play with a blind tasting on Pinot from Sonoma vs Pinot from Napa to see if you can tell the differences.

2023: The vintage or when the wine was made. In the year 2025, this is considered a young wine because it is less than 5 years old. Younger wines in the New World generally have a more fruit forward/jam aspect than older wines. Older wines are exposed to more oxygen (cork is slightly porous and micro doses oxygen into the bottle) and leans less fruity and more towards a leather wallet or almonds.

STAG'S LEAP WINE CELLARS
ARTEMIS
Cabernet Sauvignon
Napa Valley

WARREN WINIARSKI, FOUNDER

Cabernet Sauvignons from Napa Valley can be an intimidating category. If you want to understand wine, this is a classic grape from a classic region, this wine in particular is a classic producer with a chunk of important wine history. This producer is a great choice when you're at a work dinner and you're tasked with picking the wine for a group and want a great story to tell. Gather round, children.

Stag's Leap Wine Cellars: The name of the winery. My favorite fun fact is there are two Stags Leap in Napa. Both were founded in 1972, but one has an apostrophe before the seconds andone has it after the s. To be expected, they both say they came up with the name first. There was a whole lawsuit and everything, but the judge ultimately decided both were named simply after the area, so both producers still exist today. If you ever ask yourself, "Wow how does Marie know all of this?" Google is your friend. You'd be shocked how many times a sommelier will google something on the label every night. This is how we learn!

Artemis: The name of the cuvée. Wineries grow lots of grapes and make many different wines, so a cuvée is one of the wines a producer will make. This one was named after the goddess of the hunt.

How To Read A Wine Label

Cabernet Sauvignon: Name of the varietal. Its thick skins and small-sized grapes mean there's more surface area for the tannins and pigmentation to seep into the juice, allowing for some of the biggest, boldest wines in the game.

Napa Valley: The name of the wine region in Northern California, where much of American winemaking was born and home to many famous names you see on the shelf today. The valley has a cooling effect on the southern end due to the San Pablo Bay and gets warmer as you go north. This allows for a wide variety of climates and fog formation that makes the Valley a perfect place for grape growing. Some people spend their whole careers digging into the nuances and producers of Napa Valley.

Estate Winner Paris Tasting 1976: One of the most famous historical events in wine is the Judgment of Paris. In 1976 France and the US wanted to decide who made better wine, so they held a blind tasting with both French and American wine professionals to see who was better. Stag's Leap Cabernet won first place, just barely beating out Chateau Mouton-Rothschild out of Bordeaux. There's even a bottle of the winning wine, a 1973 Stag's Leap Wine Cellars 'SLV' Cabernet, in the Smithsonian today. There's a whole movie with Alan Rickman called Bottle Shock if you wanna check it out. Suck on that, France.

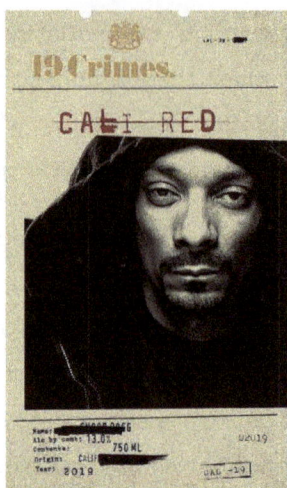

An iconic rapper and producer turned wine brand is what the New World of wine is all about. We talk about New World innovation and this is what we mean. Swapping out the gin and juice, the brand of Snoop Dogg carries the sales while its flavor profile is approachable for the American palate.

19 Crimes Cali Red: 19 Crimes is the name of the winery and Cali Red is the wine they make, which is also called the cuvée. This wine is a blend of many grapes and by state law they don't need to put in on the label. Not knowing the exact grapes does knock one of our build blockings away, but let's see if we can get any other information.

Alc by cont: 13.0%: Falls within our normal range for red wines.

Contents 750ml: A standard bottle size.

Year: 2019: The vintage of the wine

Origin: California: Lets go through our building block concepts. California, being a New World wine region, can be anticipated to have bold, fruit forward flavors. It also falls into a warm climate, which would be like a red tomato in our analogy, confirming juicy fruits. Look how much we've inferred with limited knowledge and not even knowing the grape! There is a piece on here that is not on the label but worth talking about. If you've have this wine before, it does lean a little towards the sweet side, almost like drinking cherry cola. Theres nowhere on the label (or even a search on the website) that would confirm that. I find this phenomenon does happen more with American wines than anywhere else, and is something to keep in mind. I personally find that a wine like this is a great recommendation for people who say they don't like most wine!

Wait, are we in France? Is this Champagne? Part of the innovation of the New World is that sometimes they'll pay homage to the Old World. Domaine Carneros is indeed owned by the French winery Taittinger—showing that you can perhaps expect a Champagne-like style of wine—but on domestic soils.

Picture of the domaine: That's really what it looks like, if you ever pay a visit. I personally think this is a nice touch and usually see it on Old World style labels.

Domaine Carneros by Taittinger: We live in a global world, and the New World is more likely to adopt Old World marketing than the Old World is to take on New World techniques.

TAITTINGER

Méthode Champenoise: In short, this is a sparkling wine made in the same way as Champagne, aka the Champagne Method. This method requires a bit more labor and time, and therefore falls in a higher price point and, in theory, quality level. Since this wine is not made in Champagne, France, they cannot have the word Champagne on the label—but they can put Méthode Champenoise.

How To Read A Wine Label

Brut: Meaning "dry" in French.

If I may be so forreal: Many sparkling wines under 30 bucks will be bubbly, dry, and likely tasty. When starting out, knowing the difference between sparkling wines like Champagne, crémant, Cava, and Prosecco is most important. As you get more into it, I suggest playing this game: invite some friends over for a blind tasting and have everyone pitch in on the wines. Buy two or three different sparkling wines and see if you can tell the difference. Some people won't be able to, but I think many will be surprised to notice more nuances with the different styles. If I had all the money in the world, I'd be buying Champagne.

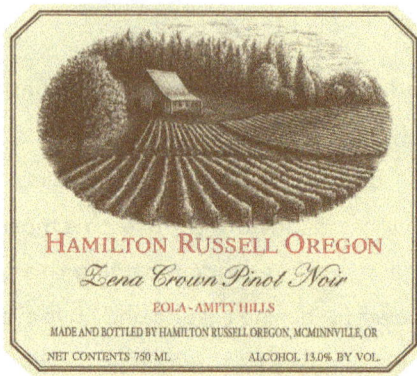

HAMILTON RUSSELL OREGON
Zena Crown Pinot Noir
EOLA-AMITY HILLS
MADE AND BOTTLED BY HAMILTON RUSSELL OREGON, MCMINNVILLE, OR
NET CONTENTS 750 ML   ALCOHOL 13.0% BY VOL.

California, New York, and Washington get the credit for producing the most wine in the country. Oregon is surprisingly under the radar for most new wine drinkers, but I'd like to change that today. Willamette Valley is a region known for people who like to ride the line of New World and Old World style, and is definitely a sommelier-favorite region.

Hamilton Russell Oregon: Name of the producer. The original Hamilton Russell Vineyards is a South African winery hence the 'Oregon' distinction.

Zena Crown Pinot Noir: These are two separate phrases "Zena Crown" and "Pinot Noir" not some hybrid Pinot Noir grape. In all honesty, it's hard to tell if Zena Crown is the vineyard site of the name of the cuvée just by looking at it. Even after some aggressive Googling it's still not clear, so don't be discouraged if you look something up and it doesn't really make sense. When this happens (and it will happen again) I'd advise moving on and focusing on what we know for sure, that this is a Pinot Noir, a thin-skinned grape that likely has a lighter body and low tannins.

Eola-Amity Hills: This is a specific region within the Willamette Valley is, you could use some context like the varietal being on the label that this is the New World. Willamette Valley is the most famous wine region in Oregon, and due to its cool to temperate climate and interesting soil composition, this is a popular destination for modern winemaking. So popular in fact, a winery from another country would come here to make wine. That's saying something!

Alc 13.0% by Vol: This is like a dry, light-bodied wine, where the alcohol level matches nicely with the varietal Pinot Noir.

FRENCH

Region & Wine You'll Find:

1 **Loire Valley**
Musacdet, Sauvignon Blanc,
Chenin Blanc

2 **Champagne**
Sparkling Wines

3 **Alsace**
Riesling, Pinto Gris,
Gewürztraminer

4 **Burgundy**
Pinot Noir, Chardonnay, Gamay

5 **Rhône Valley**
Syrah, Grenache Blends

6 **Provence**
Rose Blends

7 **Bordeaux**
Cabernet Sauvignon,
Merlot Blends

How To Read A Wine Label

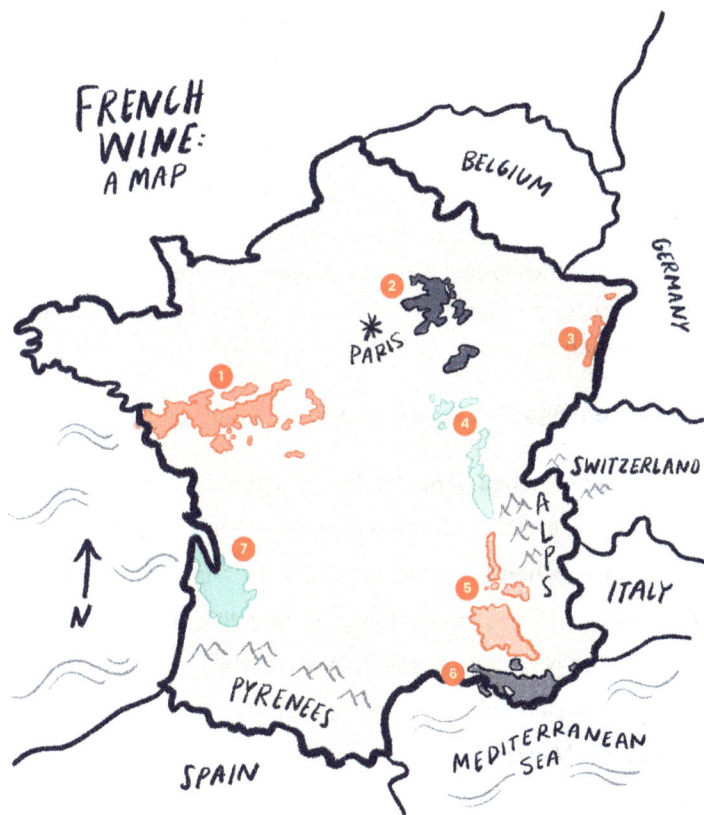

FRENCH
WINE:
A MAP

BELGIUM

GERMANY

2
☀
PARIS

3

1

4

SWITZERLAND

A
L
P
S

ITALY

N

7

5

6

PYRENEES

SPAIN

MEDITERRANEAN
SEA

FONDÉE EN 1859

BEAUJOLAIS-VILLAGES
Appellation d'Origine Contrôlée

LOUIS JADOT
BEAUNE · FRANCE

By seeing the word 'Beaujolais' you're likely drinking a red wine made from Gamay grapes. Known of light-bodied, fruity red wines, these wines are pure yo be crowd-pleasers with nots of cherries, raspberries and violets. Food-friendly and great for chugging right out of the bottle. We're starting off with a simple label to get you eased into the Old World wine label structure.

Fondée en 1859: The winery was founded in 1859.

Beaujolais-Villages Appellation d'Origine Contrôlée: The addition here of "Appellation d'Origine Contrôlée", aka AOC, should be a helpful indicator. This falls into the AOC of Beaujolais-Villages. Beaujolais is technically part of Burgundy, but has really become its own recognizable region. You'll see wines from Beaujolais that say either just plainly, Beaujolais, Beaujolais-Villages or even sometimes a very specific region called a "cru". Referring back to the Prosciutto Parable, the more specific the AOC, the higher quality/more expensive the wine will be.

Louis Jadot: The name of the producer/winemaker. They make French wines at all different quality levels and styles so they're a solid name to recognize in while shopping.

How To Read A Wine Label

Beaune, France: Although Louis Jadot gets grapes from all over Burgundy to make a bunch of different wines, their winery (where they turn grapes into wine) and cellar (where they age wine) is located in Beaune, France.

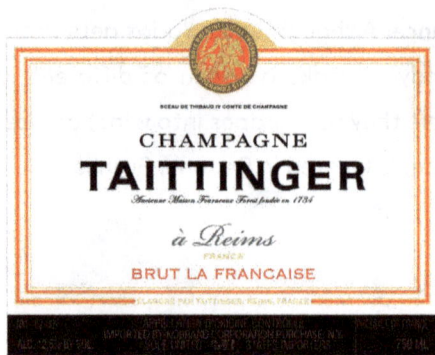

When you see "Champagne" on the label, we're tasting the crème de la crème and the best place for sparkling wine (potentially) In the world! With that said it's going to cost you, because you're paying for the small pet of taste estate in Champagne. Champagne is 99.9% sparkling wine, usually dry, and totally delicious

Sceau de Thibaud IV Comte de Champagne: This particular winemaker exercised some creative freedoms and mentioned a particular comte ("count") who was instrumental in refining the high-quality wines of Champagne. It's a pretty cool story so check out the Taittinger website for more.

Champagne Taittinger: Name of winemaker. You wouldn't be faulted for thinking these are two different things: "Champagne" for the region, and "Taittinger" as the name of the winemaker. But if you refer to number 4, you'll see this winemaker goes a bit more into detail.

Ancienne Maison Fourneaux-Forest fondée en 1734: This line states that the "ancient" Maison Fourneaux-Forest was founded in 1734. Does this tell you how the wine will taste? Not really, but it's the producer's way of paying respects to winery's history!

How To Read A Wine Label

à Reims, France: Meaning "of Reims, France". Reims is a specific area in Champagne.

Brut La Française: Taittinger makes a TON of different kinds of wines or "cuvées", all with certain percentages of grapes and sweetness levels. This particular cuvée is called "Brut La Française". If you REALLY start digging into wines you'll find yourself not only fond of a certain winemaker, but even certain cuvées.

Élaboré à Taittinger, Reims, France: Literally translates to "elaborated at Taittinger" aka made on location at Taittinger.

Alc 12.5% by vol: Alcohol percentage for sparkling wines, I like to us the white wine range of reference which we said was 11-14%. 12% falls nicely into a typical range of white wines.

Appellation d'Origine Contrôlée; Imported by Kobrand Corporation Purchase, NY; Sole United States importers: This line states the AOC as well as the importer. The importer acts as the middleman between the winemaker and the consumer (that's you!)

Product of France, 750 ml: Legally required information, 750 ml is the volume of a standard- sized bottle.

ALSACE
APPELLATION ALSACE CONTRÔLÉE

DEPUIS   DOMAINE

Domaine
Zind Humbrecht

MISE

GEWURZTRAMINER
TURCKHEIM

750 ML
ALC. 14% BY VOL
INDICE 2

OLIVIER ET MARGARET HUMBRECHT PROP.-VITIC. A TURCKHEIM (HAUT-RHIN) FRANCE

L 170

Remember when I said that Europe usually won't have the grape on the label? Welcome to the world of wine where there's undoubtedly an exception to every rule (Lord, help us). The exception is a place called Alsace in eastern France. You'll usually find the varietal on these labels and these can be a softer start for beginner wine label readers.

Alsace Appellation d'Origine Contrôlée: We found that word "Contrôlée" again. Hint, hint, this wine has met regulations to have Alsace AOC on the label, meaning it already reaches a certain level of government-mandated qualifications, i.e. it's likely to be more expensive and on a par with Alsatian exceptions of a wine.

Domaine Zind Humbrecht: The name of the producer.

Dupuis 1658: Dupuis meaning "since" 1658. So, this winery has been making wine since 1658. This is not to be confused with the vintage, which on some French labels is displayed on an extra sticker on the neck of the bottle. Some producers do this so they can use the same label every year and not have to reprint it with the appropriate vintage. But if you do ever find a 1658 vintage wine, you should definitely keep it—it would be worth thousands!

How To Read A Wine Label

Gewürztraminer: This wine is made with 100% Gewürztraminer grapes. You're very likely to find German grapes in Alsace like this one, as well as Riesling. This is due to the land of Alsace being at the whim of a game of tug-of-war between France and Germany (take a look at the French wine map from a few pages ago and see how close they are to each other). Gewürztraminer is a voluptuous white grape known for aromas of ginger, white pepper, and crisp yellow apples.

Turckheim: Turckheim is a small town located in Alsace. This particular producer creates wines from many vineyard sites around Alsace, and they have a few vineyard sites in this town. They have chosen to disclose the specific town because they believe that each vineyard has a certain style and taste, which we call "terrior". Adding the town/vineyard name on the label adds another layer of the perceived quality of a wine. For most people, this detail can be glossed over. However, you may start tasting more wines from a region you love (perhaps Alsace?) and you may start to say, "Not only do I love Alsatian white wines, I REALLY love the ones from Turckheim." If you're saying stuff like that then you're more of a nerd than I am.

Vin Sec: Meaning "dry wine" in French. This is part of another legal grading system to tell you the sweetness level of the wine. In Alsace, the least sweet is sec ("dry") and the most sweet is doux ("sweet")—wine is complicated but sometimes it just has to say what it means. Three main regions classically will tell you the sweetness level right on the wine: Alsace, Champagne, and the Loire Valley.

This label is giving Champagne *vibes*, but let's take a closer look. Is it sparkling (see "White French sparkling wine" near the bottom)? Yes. Is it from France (see "Produce of France" at the top)? Yes! But do you see the word "Champagne"? Non (French for "no").

Therefore, it's not Champagne but you've discovered something wonderful (and at a fraction of the price). Welcome to everywhere else in France that makes sparkling wine! The key here is that it says "Crémant". If you see Crémant, think: a sparkling wine not from Champagne, but made with the same amount of attention to detail.

Bouvet: The name of the producer.

Crémant de Loire: Translates to "a Crémant of Loire (Valley)". Crémant is the name for sparkling wines in Champagne that are slightly less bubbly at 4 atmospheric pressure (for reference, a car tire is 2 atmospheric pressure) than their proper Champagne (5–6 atm). And, since 1985, it has also become the term used for sparkling white wines made in the same style as Champagne, just not in the same region.

How To Read A Wine Label

Brut Excellence: Brut is a legal term meaning "dry" (there are regulated levels of dryness). On the other hand, the word excellence has no legal bearing and is used as a term to differentiate their product. Some people call this *marketing*.

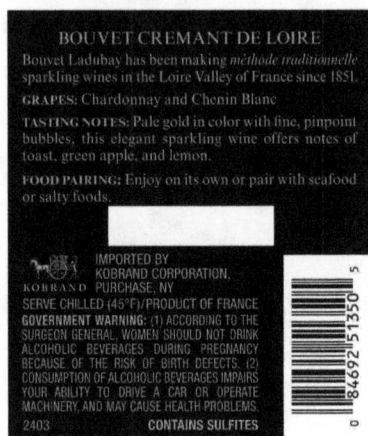

BOUVET CREMANT DE LOIRE
Bouvet Ladubay has been making *méthode traditionnelle* sparkling wines in the Loire Valley of France since 1851.

GRAPES: Chardonnay and Chenin Blanc

TASTING NOTES: Pale gold in color with fine, pinpoint bubbles, this elegant sparkling wine offers notes of toast, green apple, and lemon.

FOOD PAIRING: Enjoy on its own or pair with seafood or salty foods.

IMPORTED BY
KOBRAND CORPORATION,
KOBRAND PURCHASE, NY
SERVE CHILLED (45°F)/PRODUCT OF FRANCE
GOVERNMENT WARNING: (1) ACCORDING TO THE SURGEON GENERAL, WOMEN SHOULD NOT DRINK ALCOHOLIC BEVERAGES DURING PREGNANCY BECAUSE OF THE RISK OF BIRTH DEFECTS. (2) CONSUMPTION OF ALCOHOLIC BEVERAGES IMPAIRS YOUR ABILITY TO DRIVE A CAR OR OPERATE MACHINERY, AND MAY CAUSE HEALTH PROBLEMS.
2403   **CONTAINS SULFITES**

This is the back label of the Bouvet Crémant de Loire. Much like front labels, the back labels vary from wine to wine. In most cases, the back label will be filled with mandatory items like the US government warning and barcode. If you're lucky, you'll get a snapshot of the story of the winemaker and some more specific info about the wine. If the front label doesn't give you enough info, always check the back!

Bouvet Ladubay has been...: Some winemakers will be adamant about giving a bit of philosophy or history of their winery on the back. This back label goes above and beyond by explaining the grapes used, as well as tasting notes and food pairings. In my eyes, this label gets a 10 outta 10 *chef's kiss*.

Imported by Kobrand Corporation: This is the importer, aka the company that imports the wine from France to the US. In the US, most wines will be represented by an importer or distributor. Importers have turned into a brand themselves, and are a key to finding wines you like.

A sommelier secret: Sometimes what they don't put on a label is as important as what they do, but this requires some previous knowledge and context. Hey, that's why I'm here, right? Crémant wines are made in the same exact way as sparkling wines from Champagne, so they follow the same rules. In this case, because it's non-vintage, the year doesn't matter so they don't even include it.

VIN DE PROVENCE

AIX

APPELLATION D'ORIGINE PROTÉGÉE
COTEAUX D'AIX EN PROVENCE

VIN DE PROVENCE

AIX

PROVENCE ROSÉ WINE
AOP COTEAUX D'AIX EN PROVENCE
AIX ROSÉ IS A PREMIUM PROVENCE ROSÉ MADE
WITH DEDICATION AND PASSION. ENJOY THE NOTES
OF SOFT, RIPE SUMMER FRUITS, SUCH AS
WATERMELON AND STRAWBERRIES.

IMPORTED BY KOBRAND CORPORATION
PURCHASE, NY. SOLE US IMPORTERS
BOTTLED BY EMB 83023G POUR SARL MAISON
SAINT AIX NÉGOCIANT À JOUQUES - FRANCE

KOBRAND
FINE WINE AND SPIRITS
Since 1944

GOVERNMENT WARNING: (1) ACCORDING TO THE SURGEON
GENERAL, WOMEN SHOULD NOT DRINK ALCOHOLIC BEVERAGES DURING
PREGNANCY BECAUSE OF THE RISK OF BIRTH DEFECTS. (2) CONSUMPTION
OF ALCOHOLIC BEVERAGES IMPAIRS YOUR ABILITY TO DRIVE
A CAR OR OPERATE MACHINERY, AND MAY CAUSE HEALTH PROBLEMS.

13% ALC. BY VOL.
750ML CA CRV
CONTAINS SULFITES
PRODUCT OF FRANCE 8 59310 00600 0

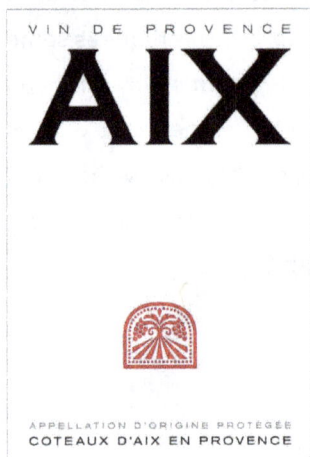

Provence = Rosé (for the most part)! Yes, they make other wines, but you'll likely associate this region with dry rosés that'll taste like pink lemonade, sandy beaches, and with more acid than a Coachella after party.

Vin de Provence: Meaning "wine of Provence"

AIX: Aix is the name of the producer, pronounced like the letter "x" (if you've been saying it wrong for years, like I have, you're not alone).

2022: The grapes were harvested in 2022. In general, wines under four years of age are considered young. Young wines will usually have flavors that reflect the fresh, fruit-forward flavors like apples, strawberries, and cherries. Older wines anywhere from five to 20 years old will have flavors that indicate some aging like toasted nuts, freshly ground coffee, and can even be reminiscent of a well-worn leather wallet.

Appellation d'Origine Protégée Coteaux d'Aix en Provence: This means this wine meets the standards to achieve AOP (a similar concept to AOC) quality in Aix-en-Provence. Rosé accounts for 91% of the wine production in Provence, and due to its coastal, Mediterranean climate, it's a certified patio pounder.

Provence Rosé Wine AOP Coteaux d'Aix en Provence: We can just translate this one directly: it's a rosé wine from Provence and it adheres to the AOP Coteaux d'Aix en Provence rules.

Aix rosé is a premium…: Some winemakers are gracious enough to give a helpful explanation of how the wine will taste and a bit about the region. I'd love to see more of this in the future from winemakers, but empowering yourself with the knowledge you'll find in this book is best!

Imported by Kobrand Corporation: The importer acts as the middleman between the winemaker and the consumer (that's you!).

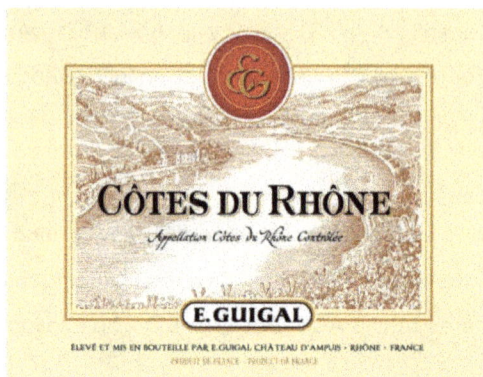

This label and the next label will play into each other nicely! They're both from the same region and mostly use the same grapes, so you'll likely see them close to each other in a wine shop. The biggest difference you'll see? The price point. Let's break it down.

EG: Initials for E. Guigal, the producer of this wine.

Picture of a flowing river in the background: Not just for show, my friends! They took some artistic direction with this, and used an illustration of their vineyards and maison (French for "house", it is usually the actual house where the vignernon/winemaker/owner lives, and they will sometimes host wine tastings there) along the Vienne river in France. You can even see the little house along the bank. Fancy!

Côtes du Rhône Appellation Côtes du Rhône Contrôlée: This wine fits the bill for satisfying all the requirements met for the AOC of this region. As we move south, we reach warmer, more Mediterranean climates. We pull away from the Pinot Noirs and move towards the big-bodied Syrah grape. Wines from this region are classically made with a blend of Syrah, Grenache, and Mourvèdre, but the main component is usually

How To Read A Wine Label

Syrah. Following the flowchart, this Old World, warm climate, and thick-skinned grapes tend towards wine with body, power, and a bit of earthy finesse. Because it's a bigger AOC, you can collect grapes from anywhere within Côtes du Rhône, which is quite a lot! With that, you're allowed access to more grapes, which means cheaper grapes, with less bottle or oak aging, and therefore you get a cheaper product.

E. Guigal: The iconic producer for the region, Guigal creates many wines at every quality level. This entry-level (when I say entry-level, this is my marketing-ish way of saying it's their cheapest option) Côtes du Rhône is easily found and has been part of professional blind-tasting groups since forever. They also create wines from even more specific sites like Côte Rôtie, which fetch a pretty penny due to real estate and the wines receiving south-facing, most-sun-having grapes. Like many French producers, Guigal uses environmentally sustainable methods of pest, disease, and weed control. Many of their higher-end wines do include a bit of new oak aging, adding a layered baking spice thing that people love. Nowhere on the label will tell you if they use oak or not, but that is something wine people will quickly google to see.

Élevé et mis en bouteille par E. Guigal, Château d'Ampuis – Rhône – France: In French it's "raised and made in bottle for E Guigal, Château d'Ampuis", meaning that the grapes were grown, made, and bottled all within their estate. Not all wineries can do this, so it's a bit of a flex to be able to put this on a label.

Produit du France ("Product of France"): If you were really struggling to work out where this wine is from, this is the most helpful hint. Knowing that this wine is from France, what sort of characteristics can we expect?

FAMILLE PERRIN

Château de Beaucastel

CHATEAUNEUF-DU PAPE
APPELLATION CHATEAUNEUF-DU-PAPE CONTROLÉE

PRODUIT DE FRANCE - PRODUCT OF FRANCE

A region most recognizable on fancy restaurant lists, Châteauneuf (meaning "new castle") got its name from John Pope XXII who built a castle on the hill in the area. Ye olde marketing team saw the financial potential of the Pope's zip code and added the "du-Pape" to Châteauneuf in 1893. At higher quality levels, you'll see the keys to the Kingdom of Heaven given to Saint Peter embossed on the bottle itself. I wonder if they'll open the wine cellar...

Famille Perrin: Translates to "Family Perrin" or the family that makes the wine. Many historic wineries are family-owned for generations and providing the name reenforces the traditional aspects of Old World winemaking culture. In France, the word vigneron may be used and has a bit more weight to it because it means you're cultivating and making the wine (this is becoming less common these days). The French wouldn't be too mad if you called them a winemaker, but the most accurate word would be *vigneron*.

Château de Beaucastel: In its serif-fonted glory, this is the name of the winemaker.

Châteauneuf-du-Pape: A region that is shockingly warm compared to the rest of France, it's actually situated right next to Provence and shares a more Mediterranean climate. Home of other famous regions like Côte Rôtie ("the roasted slope"... because it's hot, get it?) means that it's giving red tomato in our tomato analogy. You're getting big-bodied, richer wines, but being in the Old World means we're still getting earthy notes like a pack of Jack Link's peppered beef jerky. If the Pope left his primary Vatican City home, you'd imagine that he would want to live in a similar climate with a palm tree or two. Châteauneuf-du-Pape is a region within Côtes du Rhône, so we're working with a smaller area in which to collect grapes. Fewer grapes = you can charge more money. Another fun fact is that this region is special due to a specific type of soil called *galets roulés* ("rolled pebbles"), which is thought to be integral to the growth of vines and, more importantly, the ripening of the fruit by absorbing the heat from the daytime sunshine, and then releasing that heat slowly overnight due to the soil's natural capacity for heat retention and transmission. People pay big bucks to be on these sites!

Appellation Châteauneuf-du-Pape Contrôlée: This wine falls into the quality criteria to be able to put this on the label. This requires usage of specific grapes, the grapes to come from the right places, and legally standardized aging times. You'll classically find the blend of grapes Grenache, Mourvèdre, and Syrah, which people abbreviate to "GSM". This region falls into the Côtes du Rhône, but it's a specific place in Côtes du Rhône, so it's a higher quality level, and therefore costs more dollars. Having this on a label is their way of saying, "Don't worry, we're legit."

Sancerre

Appellation Sancerre Contrôlée

Mise en bouteille au Domaine

Hippolyte Reverdy propriétaires Chaudoux-Verdigny
et ses fils viticulteurs -Cher-

WHITE WINE   PRODUCE OF FRANCE   750 ML
ALC. 13% BY VOL.   CONTAINS SULFITES
IMPORTED BY KERMIT LYNCH WINE MERCHANT   BERKELEY, CA.

I love these J.R.R. Tolkien (my second *Lord of the Rings* reference in this book...) inspired labels. It makes me want to adventure, and drink wine, and eat a turkey leg. Where's my lute? Anyways, Sancerre is a winemaking region in the Loire Valley in France. Situated nicely along the Loire River, the Loire Valley was prime real estate for Parisians' second vacation home. The equivalent of the Hamptons to New York City dwellers, if you will.

Sancerre Appellation Sancerre Contrôlée: They sure are PROUD of being from Sancerre, can't you tell? Plastering the place on the top of the label is very Old World of them. This is one of those cases where you must know the name of the region and relate it to a grape. If you were born in France, you may not know white Sancerre is Sauvignon Blanc and would just say you like Sancerre, but for everyone else it is helpful to know that Sancerre is Sauvignon Blanc. These savvy b's have a tart lemon zip with distinct minimality that's giving babbling brook and earthy undertones. Vastly different from our New World caution blancs classically from New Zealand or California.

Mise en bouteille au Domaine Hippolyte Reverdy et Ses Fils: Reverdy and sons is the name of the winemaker.

Imported by Kermit Lynch Wine Merchant Berkeley, CA: Our importer! The importer brings wine into the United States. Kermit Lynch is one of the OG wine importers in America, so I certainly trust them. Some recommended reading would be On The Wine Route by Kermit Lynch himself, which helped me pique my interest in wine when I first started out.

All 13% by Vol: Within our typical range for white wines.

CHÂTEAU
LA GAFFELIÈRE

1ᵉʳ GRAND CRU CLASSÉ

SAINT·ÉMILION GRAND CRU

Comte de Malet Roquefort

Tread carefully, dear Watson. Bordeaux is generally where people's eyes glaze over when I talk about wine. There are a gazillion RULES based on historical events and these rules determine the quality levels that, most importantly, determine the price and, secondly, determine the flavor. Let's start with a simple label so as not to scare you away.

Château La Gaffelière: Whew, okay, easy start, the name of the winemaker. It won't tell us much about how the wine will taste, but it's nice to know.

1er Grand Cru Classé: This is an official classification of quality within a standard set in Bordeaux called the 1855 Classification. This classification was established during the 1855 Paris World Fair at the request of the Napoleon alive at the time. This ranking was based on the actual wine value in the trading market, and this producer was one of the wines in this ranking. People generally pay more money for wines with "Grand Cru Classé" on the label because Napoleon liked it.

Saint-Émilion Grand Cru: Bordeaux isn't a big place, but it is a significant place. It's so jam- packed with regulations, and nuance, and soil types that it has been divided into small sections. These sections are called "villages". Saint-Émilion is the name of one of these villages, located on the eastern side of the Garonne river. This river has significance because the soil types change dramatically, and professionals will tell you there's a big difference in taste across these wines. Everyday drinkers may tell you a different story. These nuances and discussion about quality within Saint-Émilion led to the creation of their own quality system. It unfortunately doesn't end there—there is even a difference between the Saint-Émilion classification system vs the Saint- Émilion Grand Cru classification system. Bordeaux is like a fractal, infinitely complex, but the complexity comes from simplicity in a way, with the simple goal for the pursuit of excellent wine. Bordeaux is full of craftspeople who are obsessed with making the perfect bottle of Bordeaux. This drives the price as infinitely high as its fractal ideology. I don't know what kind of people look into the eyes of God and create something like this.

Meursault

APPELLATION MEURSAULT CONTRÔLÉE

BURGUNDY WHITE WINE

MIS EN BOUTEILLE PAR

Thierry et Pascale Matrot

A F-21190 CÔTE-D'OR - FRANCE

PRODUCT OF FRANCE

Alc. 13% by vol.

750 ml

CONTAINS SULFITES (E220)

Burgundy, baby—she's a legend, she's an icon, and she has been of the moment for the past millennium. Beaujolais is technically part of Burgundy, so they're basically siblings. But Beaujolais is more likely to smoke weed by the river, while Burgundy is more likely to throw a house party and drink wine out of their parents cellar. People who get into Burgundy tend to fall into a rabbit hole. I could go on for an entire book about Burgundy, but that's not what this book is about!

Grand Vin de Bourgogne: "Great wine of Burgundy." This is not a term regulated by the AOC and holds no quality distinction, but is a term that wineries tend to put on wines. It does not indicate a particular quality level, but there is a useful word on their Bourgogne, the French word meaning "Burgundy". You'll find the term "Bourgogne" on cheaper Burgundies that do not fit within AOC or high-quality guidelines. If you like this wine, but wanna spend a bit less, look for the word "Bourgogne" instead of the village name like "Meursault" or "Gevrey-Chambertin"!

Meursault: A village/appellation within Burgundy. There are 44 notable villages within Burgundy, and when you're starting out it's hard to remember any distinct details about any of them. Luckily there's great news for beginners: in Burgundy, if the wine is red it's going to be Pinot Noir. If it's a white wine, it's almost always going to be Chardonnay. Not many rules are this simple, so let's just take that win where we can get it.

Appellation Meursault Contrôlée: Some villages in Burgundy are more well known for their reds and some their whites. This is a personal favorite village when I get to break open my "emergency wine" piggy bank. These Chardonnays are complex, layered, and taste radically different from when you first open it to sipping the last glass. I joke that it's like getting two wines for the price of one.

Burgundy white wine: They won't always spell it out for you in plain English, but they do here! Nicely affirms everything else we've speculated about the label. If it's a white wine in Burgundy, it's Chardonnay, if it's a red wine, it's Pinot Noir.

Mis en Bouteille par Thierry et Pascale Matrot: "Made in bottle by the winemakers." Kinda interesting that they highlight the village in bigger letters than the producer. This is more standard in Burgundy because to name the village is to put the terrior and the wine first over the winemaker. A surprising lack of ego is always refreshing in wine.

Alc 13% by vol: Fits nicely into our 11–14% bracket for white wines, meaning that this will be a more expected cooler-climate, lighter-bodied Chardonnay.

A F-21190 Côte-d'Or – France: A code used for AOC purposes along with a more general region of Burgundy called the "Gold Coast" or Côte-d'Or (pronounced "coat door").

750 ml: A standard-size bottle of wine.

Contains sulfites (E220): Our standard legal obligation, but with something more! E220 is the European code for the preservative, sulfur dioxide (SO_2). SO_2 is naturally occurring within the winemaking process, but can also be added by the winemaker to maintain freshness (especially for overseas shipping). Pretty much all wines will have this label on them.

The label that inspired me to write this book, THE SPACE CATS. A label that is fun and eye-catching, but you have absolutely no idea how it's going to taste... until now! Let's see if we can glean anything from the back label about what the wine may taste like.

In 1983 Felicette...: A harrowing story of space travel and never letting your dreams die. It won't tell you how the wine tastes, but I always enjoy a story on a label.

2019: The vintage or when the wine was made.

Grenache Rouge: In this example let's pretend I'm not helping you. What do you think this is? The region or the grape, perhaps? Maybe it has a similar name to a regional grape we just went over in this section?

Pays d'Oc Indication Géographique Protégée: Good Lord, more words we don't know! It's okay that you don't know what Pays d'Oc is or even what IGP means, but you can probably take a stab that it sounds pretty French.

How To Read A Wine Label

Produced and bottled for Maison d'Alliance – France: We've done it! Our first major clue on what the wine might taste like! We're in Europe, which is the Old World. Meaning that the wines from France will be more tart fruit and earthy than fruit forward, plus most of France is a cooler climate, so it's likely to have some zip and acid to it. Knowing this wine is from France, you might google Pays d'Oc and find out exactly where it is in France! Your journey to knowing about wine has begun.

Product of France: Just in case you missed it the first time, this is a product of France.

Alc 13.5% by vol: Falls nicely into the normal range for red wines and maybe even on the lower side. This tells us that the wine might resemble more of a Pinot Noir or Gamay.

Contains sulfites: Big surprise! This wine has sulfites because almost all wine has sulfites.

A note: This is my actual thought process when I look at new labels and I don't recognize the classic grapes or regions. Stick to what you know from the building blocks we've learned about before making assumptions about the wine. Just by reading the label, you should be able to connect the dots and work out that this might be similar to a Beaujolais or even a Sangiovese from Italy. Of course, the only way to truly find out is to drink it (maybe pay for it first though). Space cats FTW.

La Vieille Ferme

Mis en bouteille par la Vieille Ferme

750 ml   Appellation Ventoux Contrôlée
Vin rouge • Red wine   13,5% alc/vol
13,5% vol.

I'm trying to drive home the point that cute labels have something to tell you about what the wine might taste like based on region, climate, and grapes. Some things are inferred, and some are explicitly put on the label. I hope it's starting to feel like math problems with your dad, and that you're saying, "Okay, I get it, please stop!!" But we shall not stop. We have just begun.

Vignobles de la Vallée du Rhône: Meaning vignobles aka winemakers of the Rhône Valley. You can find The Chicken Wine all over the world, which means they have to produce a ton of it. To do this, the winemakers get grapes from from different farmers and winemakers within a more generalized region. If we think about a more specific place suggesting a higher quality and price point, then the opposite would be true. My Midwestern sensibilities understand that I don't want to spend $40 bucks on a bottle of wine every time. Sometimes I just want a cheeseburger. Sometimes I just want Chicken Wine. There's a time and place for everything, and theres always a place for Chicken Wine.

La Vieille Ferme: Meaning "the old farm", this is the name of the winery.

Chickens: These cute little guys are the marketing move of the century. Affectionately called The Chicken Wine in the US, it's an extremely clever way for people to feel comfortable talking about this wine without dancing around pronouncing La Vieille Ferme correctly.

Appellation Ventoux Contrôlée: This is one of those things where I can tell if you're going to buy 10 more wine books after reading this book. If you read this label and said, "WTF is Ventoux?" Give it Google, you'll find that it's a specific AOC within Vallée du Rhone. The Tour De France goes through it, and it has a specific mesoclimate, culture, and biodiversity. Each and every wine region is like this. This book is here to whet your whistle and either help you survive the wine aisle or open a whole new world. If you said, "I just like the chicken wine," that's cool too.

13.5% alc/vol: If you were uncertain about the grapes and region thus far, this might be your helpful hint. This percentage tells you this is likely a lighter to medium bodied red wine. Add that with the knowledge that this is an Old World wine and you'll have your answer what this wine may taste like without opening it.

ITALY

Region & Wine You'll Find:

1 **Tuscany**
Sangiovese

2 **Trentino/Alto Adige**
Pinot Grigio

3 **Piedmonte**
Nebbiolo

4 **Sicily**
Nero D'Avola & Narello
Mascelese Blends

5 **Prosecco**
Sparkling Wines

6 **Abruzzo**
Montepulciano,
Trebbiano, Pecorino

SWITZERLAND

AUSTRIA

HUNGARY

ALPS

②

SLOVENIA

⑤

FRANCE

CROATIA

③

✳MILAN

BOSNIA
+
HERZEGOVINA

CORSICA

APPENNINE

①

MOUNTAINS

⑥

ADRIATIC
SEA

✳ROME

SARDINIA

TYRRHENIAN
SEA

MEDITERRANEAN
SEA

④

MT.
ETNA▲

ITALIAN
WINE:
A MAP

N

Ah, Prosecco. It's famously known for incorrectly being called Champagne at your friend's baby shower. The choice of bubbly for airlines across the world. It has all the enjoyment of sparkling wine for the most reasonable price on the shelf. Even on this producer's website they ENCOURAGE you to mix these wines to make a cocktail. My kind of people.

La Marca: The name of the producer. By this point you'll realize that the producer is mentioned on every label, but many of them have a deeper meaning to their name and La Marca is a great example of this. La Marca Trevigiana is a region in Italy, where the grapes for the wine are grown. Trevigiana is an Italian noun that means "inhabitant or native of Treviso." Treviso is in the heart of Veneto (see Italian map on the page before) and La Marca pays homage to the famous town of Prosecco within Treviso, which makes—you guessed it—Prosecco. It's always worth an extra google to see if the producer's name holds more weight than simply passing along the family name.

Prosecco DOC: Much like the French put AOC on their label to indicate that quality standards were met, the Italians put DOC after the region's name. Uniquely, Italian wines will also

How To Read A Wine Label

have a tag on the top of the bottle to indicate DOC or DOCG (a higher level of quality). Keep in mind we are still in the Old World, aka Europe, and in a cooler-climate region, which leans towards a zippier, tart, fruit-forward style that makes a great pairing for all sorts of food.

Sparkling wine: This is a sparkling wine (duh).

Product of Italy: If you didn't pick up on the hints that Prosecco is in Italy and the DOC banner on the top of the bottle is only for Italian wines, they make it nice and clear for you.

Where's the vintage? I'm gonna throw something a bit more advanced at you because I think you're starting to get the hang of this whole reading-a-wine-label thing. Sometimes when a wine withholds information like the vintage, that can also hint at something. Prosecco comes in both vintage and non-vintage (NV) styles. A vast majority of the Proseccos that come into the US are NV and it is not required by the DOC to put NV on a label, so many wineries won't do it. What would pique the interest of some wine experts would be to actually find a vintage on the label! I would say "whoa a vintage Prosecco, that's kinda cool, I've never seen that before." When you start asking more questions, what is or is not on the label will inform a deeper understanding of what makes a wine special. If anyone happens to find a vintage Prosecco, hit me up and we'll drink it together.

The white wine of all white wines: Pinot Grigio. This is usually baby's first wine, or the first wine your parents let you have at the dinner table when you were a teenager. Light, refreshing, high acid, it checks all the boxes for easy drinking. The Italian lemonade, if you will (and I will).

Ecco Domani Italia: The name of the winemaker. They could've gone hard on the marketing with a 2024 brat summer campaign with their color scheme, but I digress.

2017: The year the grapes were harvested. If we're being real, the vintage isn't super important for wineries making large quantities of wine. The more wine you have to make, the less you're likely you are to taste vintage variations—like if it was a hot, cold, rainy, or a perfect year. How do I know they make a ton of wine? Generally, if you can find it at a big-box store like Target or Walgreens, that means they make enough wine to meet the demands of those stores. Meaning that's a lotta wine.

How To Read A Wine Label

Pinot Grigio delle Venezie: Sorta interesting that this label is a combination of both the varietal (so New World of them) and the location of delle Venezie (so Old World of them). Delle Venezie is actually a culmination of many northern regions of Italy—mainly Veneto, Friuli-Venezia Giulia, and Trentino-Alto Adige—and is the largest DOC in Italy. This wine is 100% Pinot Grigio with no aging requirements, meaning you won't get any oaky flavors here.

Denominazione di Origine Controllata: Challenging. Italian. Scary. These words can be used to describe Tony Soprano or your thoughts while reading this part of the label. Let's just take the first letter of each word: D O C (di just means "of", so it's not included in the acronym). We know what a DOC is! This part reaffirms that we're in the delle Venezie DOC and the standards have been met.

Alc 12.5% by vol: Falls in line with 11–14% alcohol for a cooler-climate white wine, so affirms this will be an expectedly zippy wine.

DaVinci.

CHIANTI

2024

CHIANTI

DENOMINAZIONE DI ORIGINE
CONTROLLATA E GARANTITA

ALC. 13.5% BY VOL.

DaVinci.

CHIANTI

DENOMINAZIONE DI ORIGINE
CONTROLLATA E GARANTITA

THE TOWN OF VINCI IS HOME TO THE WORLD CLASS
WINES OF CANTINE LEONARDO DA VINCI. THE VINEYARDS
ARE NESTLED BETWEEN FLORENCE, PISA, AND SIENA IN
THE CHIANTI REGION OF TUSCANY.
CANTINE LEONARDO DA VINCI PRODUCES OUTSTANDING
WINES FROM HILLSIDE VINEYARDS TENDED FOR
GENERATIONS. EXPERTLY CRAFTED, DAVINCI CHIANTI IS
CRIMSON RED WITH INTENSE AROMAS OF RIPE FRUIT AND
HINTS OF FRESH STRAWBERRY AND PLUM.

WWW.DAVINCIWINE.COM • 1-888-871-9463
VINTED AND BOTTLED BY CANTINE LEONARDO DAVINCI SOC. AGR. COOP.
VINCI-ITALIA. • IMPORTED BY DAVINCI USA, HEALDSBURG, CA • PRODUCT
OF ITALY • CONTAINS SULFITES / CONTIENE SOLFITI • RED WINE •

750 mL ALC. 13.5% BY VOL. ℮

GOVERNMENT WARNING: (1) ACCORDING TO
THE SURGEON GENERAL, WOMEN SHOULD NOT
DRINK ALCOHOLIC BEVERAGES DURING PREG-
NANCY BECAUSE OF THE RISK OF BIRTH DE-
FECTS. (2) CONSUMPTION OF ALCOHOLIC BEV-
ERAGES IMPAIRS YOUR ABILITY TO DRIVE A
CAR OR OPERATE MACHINERY, AND MAY CAUSE
HEALTH PROBLEMS.

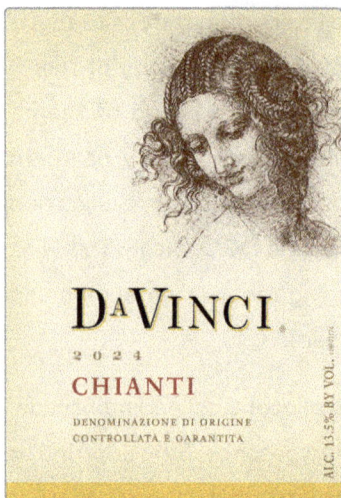

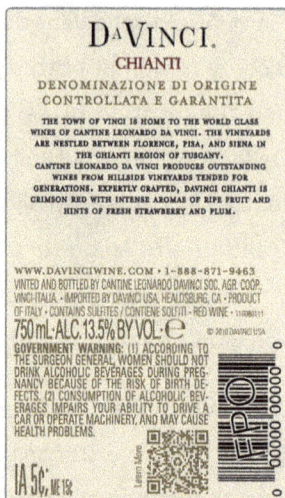

Chianti, Italy: A premium honeymoon destination. It has something that appeals to everyone, beautiful beach towns, authentic bowl of carbonara, or settings from their favorite movie Under the Tuscan Sun; another highlight is the amazing wine culture. Most people will start their wine journey in Tuscany, particularly the region of Chianti. So, let's channel our inner Julia Roberts for our Eat, Pray, Love moment in Italy's most popular wine destination.

Da Vinci: Da Vinci is a wine cooperative in the region of Chianti in Tuscany. Cooperatives are popular business models in Italy, and it means many winemakers in the region band together to share space, equipment, and profits (having all this by yourself is expensive!). You wouldn't learn this by simply looking at the label, but a quick Google will fill you in. Being a cooperative is an efficient way to make a lot of wine, or you can even choose to have a more specialized product like this one. It generally doesn't affect the flavor or quality of a wine, but many cooperatives make financially accessible wines along with a small selection of high-quality options.

Chianti: Chianti is the place and the grape is Sangiovese. Technically, it can be 95% Sangiovese and 5% of an additional local varietal. Chianti is known for a temperate Mediterranean climate, along with a great diurnal shift, which means it gets nicely warm in the day and cool at night. Grapes LOVE a diurnal shift, and many great wine regions also share this Phenomenon.

Denominazione di Origine Controllata e Garantita (DOCG): The highest level of quality found in Italy.

Riserva: Not all Chiantis will have this, but Riserva is a further quality indication level. This means this wine has seen some extra aging in the barrel (Riserva requires a minimum of two years aging; regular "Chianti" only requires a few months). Not all barrels are made the same! Barrels in Italy, for the most part, are made with a more neutral oak, which doesn't impart much flavor but does slowly introduce oxygen due to the porous nature of oak. As opposed to American oak, which makes a wine more buttery or vanilla-y. We can expect a bit more complexity and perhaps tannin with this wine.

2024: Older wines aren't always necessarily better, but the vintage of a wine does give some indication on how a wine will taste. Young wines like this one (less than 5 years old) tend to have fresh fruit flavors like berries and citrus, along with sharp acidity and grippy tannins. Aged wines (6+ years) trade fresh fruit for notes of leather, forest floor, and nuts. Not all wines benefit from aging and most wines are meant to drink young. The best agers like Bordeaux, Barolo, and

Rieslings transform dramatically with time. This Chianti plays nice as a younger or older wine.

Alc 13.5% by vol: Most Chiantis run from 13.0–14%, so this would be considered a typical alcohol percentage for the region.

Fattoria Moretto

LAMBRUSCO GRASPAROSSA DI CASTELVETRO

VINO FRIZZANTE SECCO

Imported by Kermit Lynch

Vignaioli in Castelvetro

Italians sure have a knack for making wines that taste great with their food, and Lambrusco is no exception. Lambrusco is a fruity, slightly sweet, and semi-sparkling usually red wine made in the Emilia-Romagna region. This region is known for ubiquitous Italian favorites such as Parmigiano Reggiano and Prosciutto di Parma (from the parable!). They say "if it grows together, it goes together" when it comes to wine-and-food pairings, and I think they started saying that because of Emilia-Romagna. Who's hungry?

Lambrusco Grasparossa di Castelvetro: While some Lambruscos will simply say "Lambrusco," these winemakers wanted to specificy the region near Modena called Lambrusco Grasparossa di Castelvetro. If you're a beginner, just focus that the bottle that says "Lambrusco" ANYWHERE on it—it's likely the dark-purple bubbly wine you love from the region. If you want to get granular, the DOP (think of this as one level below DOC) is called Lambrusco Grasparossa di Castelvetro, with Lambrusco Grasparossa being the specific type of grape. The intention here is to highlight the regional style of

Lambrusco, and not just pigeonhole it into a singular thing. This wine's got terrior baby!

Fattoria Moretto: Name of the winemaker.

Vino frizzante secco: Literally "wine fizzy dry". With English syntax applied, this means "a lightly bubbly dry wine." "Frizzante" is a word you'll see often in Italian wines. Frizzantes have fewer bubbles than Champagne and Prosecco, but just enough to create a fun little sensation.

Imported by Kermit Lynch: He's back! The importer Kermit Lynch is known to put their signature right on the front of the label. We'll learn more about importers near the end of the book.

Vignaioli in Castelvetro: The word vignaioli has a bit more cultural weight in Italy, but in essence this is the "winemaker"— or the "vigneron" in French. Vignaioli is an independent person who plants, tends, and harvests the vines, and then makes the wine in an artisanal way. Some would argue that most wineries do this, but it's worth exploring the nuance if it interests you! Castelvetro is the region within Emilia-Romagna.

Vietti

RISERVA
BAROLO
DENOMINAZIONE DI ORIGINE CONTROLLATA E GARANTITA

14.5% Vol.

Barolo is one of those great wine regions in Piedmont, located in northern Italy, which frequently makes its way onto restaurant wine lists and shelves in high-end wine shops. Made mainly from the Nebbiolo grape, these wines are light in color and body but enormous in tannin. They are perfect for keeping in your cellar for a decade—or, if you're drinking one today, a quick decant will help those tannins unfurl into a thing of beauty.

Vietti: Name of the winemaker. Vietti offer lots of wines at many different price points, and I find these wines at grocery stores and small wine shops alike! After a quick google I found out this is from Castiglione Falletto. This is why I like wine labels; these little nuggets, which are seemingly unimportant, can have a strong influence on what piques your interest. Castiglione Falletto means "Falletto Castle" in Italian, which is an actual castle in the region of the same name! We don't have a lot of castles in the Midwest so perhaps I find this more charming than the average Italian might. These castles usually sit on a hill and are a visual marker for the region—like a beacon for a fast travel point in a Zelda game. You'll find "Castiglione" on many Italian wine labels because of this.

Riserva: Much like Chianti, not all Barolos have this on the label. Riserva is a higher quality indication level for the region, indicating that these Barolos will have spent longer in oak, which adds complexity to the wine and demands a higher price point due to resources and time used.

Barolo: A specific region within Piedmont in northern Italy. Classically known the for thin- skinned grape Nebbiolo. If you remember from our building blocks chart, Nebbiolo is light bodied and light in color, but contains a high amount of the cotton-mouth-inducing tannins.

Alc 14.5% by vol: This is on the back label, but I still wanted to bring it up. It's technically within range for red wines, but on the highest end of our spectrum. It may feel contradictory that a thin- skinned, lighter-bodied grape has a big alcohol level, which would make the wine richer. How does this influence taste? With the grape, oak, and alcohol levels being our hints, this wine is inherently complex! There are many factors contributing to the final flavor and it can be a bit of a gamble on exactly what you're going to get. The high tannins, oak usage, and higher alcohol would tell me this is best for cellaring or drinking alongside a rich, fatty steak. Tannin and fat are friends!

Cantina Zaccagnini
il vino "dal tralcetto"
Montepulciano d'Abruzzo
denominazione di origine controllata

Red Wine

Bottled by Azienda Agricola Conte Zaccagnini s.r.l di Marcello Zaccagnini - Società Agricola in Bolognano-Pe Italia - Product of Italy

Net Cont. 750 ml   13% Alc. by vol.

Affectionately called "twig wine" or "stick wine", most people associate this wine with the vine clipping tied with hay on the bottle. This clever marketing move makes the wine stand out by adding an organic component and helps to remind people, "Wine comes from a plant, remember?" By doing this they also put one of my favorite, lesser-known regions on the map: Abruzzo, Italy.

Cantina Zaccagnini: Cantina means "cellar" or "winery" in Italian, and Zaccagnini is the family name.

Il vino "dal tralcetto": Italian for "the wine from a small branch". A nod to the real vine clipping that they tie to every bottle with a piece of hay.

Montepulciano d'Abruzzo denominazione di origine controllata: As with most European wines, the region is one of the biggest highlights on this label. This region is interesting because it includes the name of the grape in the region itself (how meta!). Montepulciano is a thin-skinned red wine grape hailing from the Abruzzo region in Italy. So, it's quite literal in the name of Montepulciano d'Abruzzo ("de"—or "d'" if it comes before a vowel—means "of"). Pronounce it like "Mon-tay-pull-chee-on-oh DA-bru-zso"—instead of "De Abruzzo"—to sound a bit more local.

13% alc by vol: Let's say you didn't google Montepulciano and you have no idea what this wine is. We can go back to our building blocks: the Old World geography plus the alcohol content are clues to guide you in the direction of 13% being within range but on the lighter/lower end of the spectrum. If you flip a few pages back to the Chianti you'll see it's .5% away from the Chianti! Using that, you might be able to guess that if you like lighter Old World reds like Chiantis, you might like this wine too.

How To Read A Wine Label

How To Read A Wine Label

OTHER WINES YOU'LL FIND

MOHUA

SAUVIGNON BLANC

NEW ZEALAND WINE

We're breaking out of specific countries and diving into a recognizable hodgepodge of wines from here on out. Starting with a favorite of mother-in-laws everywhere, New Zealand* Sauvignon Blanc makes up 71% of the country's total wine production and accounts for 85% of all wine exported from the country. Voted to be "most likely to be called 'zippy'" in high school, it's gained popularity with mother-in-laws everywhere. That's a lotta savvy b.

Marlborough: Most of the wine you'll see from Aotearoa New Zealand (ANZ) comes from the winemaking region of Marlborough, which is located on the north-eastern tip of New Zealand's South Island. This region is a real Goldilocks of not too rainy, soil with good drainage, not too hot during the day, and not too cold at night. Hence why you'll see most wines from New Zealand come from this region. We are firmly in the New World with this wine, so expect bold, fruit-forward, and intense flavors. You my think an island would have an inherently warm climate, but not here! New Zealand is a cool climate region which gives it its characteristic 'zippy' nomenclature found in wine lists everywhere.

Mohua: The name of the producer and an ode to the small black and yellow bird which can be found on the winery. Classified as an endangered species. I think one of the biggest is its use for twist-off caps instead of corks. This is a common feature for wines from Australia and ANZ, but make no mistake, there is no decrease in quality just because it has a screw cap. It really just shows that it's for drinking today instead of holding it in your cellar (aka your refrigerator door). Sauvignon Blanc: The most popular grape to come out of ANZ. A distinct characteristic of Sauvignon Blanc specifically from the New World is that it has a particular flavor that Old World Sauvignon Blancs (like those from Sancerre) don't have. It's a strong, grapefruit rind and freshly cut grass aroma that makes it distinct. Some people find this polarizing, so much so that in Sommelier school they use the phrase 'cat pee and guava tree' to describe these Sauvignon Blancs.

New Zealand Wine: If you were struggling to figure out where in the world Marlborough is, here is your definitive answer.

* There has been a national push from The Māori Party to use the native word 'Aotearoa' for the country instead of 'New Zealand'. I tend to see the usage of 'New Zealand' from bigger producers and "Aotearoa New Zealand" from smaller, bespoke wineries as a way to gently welcome in the new verbiage without confusing people.

Other Wines You'll Find

RESERVA

Muga

RIOJA
DENOMINACION DE ORIGEN CALIFICADA

Bodegas Muga S.L.
EMBOTELLADO EN LA PROPIEDAD
HARO–ESPAÑA

Bold, hot, and rich are words you could use to describe a new contestant on The Bachelor or Spain's most famous wine region, Rioja. These wines are generally made with Tempranillo, but are often blended with lesser-known, regional grapes like Garnacha and Graciano. Rioja has a warm climate spotted with cooler microclimates. They usually produce wines around 14% alcohol, giving them a ripe, big-bodied profile. People who like Napa Valley Cabernets tend to like these bad boys.

Reserva: You might have caught on by now, but if a wine says Reserve/Reserva it means the wine spends some time in oak barrels. The time and type of barrel is dependent on the region, but a Spanish Reserva has to spend a minimum of three years in barrel and use a blend of French and American Oak. Without diving in too deep, American oak gives off that oaky flavor of spices and even dried dill, while European and French oak gives a more neutral flavor but adds a light complexity. I've seen Master Sommeliers blind taste Reserva Riojas and call them New World wines due to the amount of oak they could taste.

How To Read A Wine Label

Muga: The name of the producer. This wine is Muga's flagship wine, meaning this is their signature wine that fully displays their style and winemaking techniques. You wouldn't necessarily know by looking at it, but these are the things I tend to research and find helpful if I want to determine what a classic-tasting wine from a particular region tastes like. It means I can know what's unusual or out of the ordinary in the future.

Unfiltered: Here's a little winemaking 101: squish grapes in a bucket, add yeast, wait, strain the seeds and skins from the juice, and bottle the wine. There are about 1,000 decisions at each point in this process, but this label defines something specific in the straining and filtering portion. Some wineries choose to leave their wines unfiltered, which gives the wine a distinct flavor and texture.

Other Wines You'll Find

CATENA
MALBEC

3ª GENERACIÓN   4ª GENERACIÓN

MENDOZA · ARGENTINA

Malbec, specifically from Argentina, is many people's first foray into red wine when they want something just a little different from Pinot Noir or Cabernet. It's red wine... but different!

Catena: Name of the winemaker. If you peek below the picture of the pyramid structure, you can see that there are two generations running the winery today! The full winery name is Bodega Catena Zapata, which means "House Catena Zapata". The current, fourth-generation winemaker is Laura Catena, overseen by her dad, Nicolás Catena Zapata.

Malbec: A thick-skinned grape you'll find all over the world, but classically in Mendoza, Argentina.

Building and mountains: You noticed the fabulous châteaux on the French labels, but this is a unique winery design that was inspired by Mayan architecture. Some would argue that this doesn't affect the flavor of the wine but, in my opinion, some context and a unique feature may be the ultimate decision to buy a wine. They also made a point of putting the Andes Mountains in the background, a feature that makes Mendoza particularly perfect for winemaking. The Andes separate Chile from Argentina, and just west of the mountain range you have Chile's capital Santiago, which is known for hot, dry summers, and mild, wet winters. The Andes create a topological phenomenon called a rain shadow, which separates a hot, wet Chile and stops most weather systems in their tracks, creating a more arid climate with hot days and cool nights in Mendoza. These hot days and cool nights are called diurnal shifts and some of the best wine regions in the world also benefit from rain shadows, like Central Otago in New Zealand, and Alsace in France.

Mendoza – Argentina: The wine region. Argentina is located in the New World, which we would associate with bolder, fruit-forward flavors. The caveat is that Argentina is a huge country with many different climates, so it's good to know that Mendoza is actually a cooler-climate region that is affected by the rain shadow mentioned earlier as well as its high altitude.

DR. LOOSEN

2023

Blue Slate

Riesling Kabinett

PRÄDIKATSWEIN · PRODUCE OF GERMANY
ERZEUGERABFÜLLUNG WEINGUT DR. LOOSEN · D-54470 BERNKASTEL/MOSEL
A.P. NR. 2 576 162 36 24 · ENTHÄLT SULFITE

Alc. 8.0%/Vol.   Mosel   750 ml e

By far the most intimidating labels in the entire wine world: German wines. To go over everything would be a heavy dose of explanations, so I'll go over the basics with some helpful tools to let you know if this wine will be sweet or not.

Riesling Kabinett: Riesling is the name of the most famous white grape to come from Germany. Kabinett is a quality level, similar to AOC or DOC, of wine made from Riesling. Unlike the AOC/DOCs, they do not get their designation just from being grown in a certain area, but from something unique to Germany. Back in the 1970s when Germany was a bit colder, it was quite a flex for a winemaker to be able to ripen grapes fully on the vine before harvesting. Usually, some storm or snow or hail would destroy your crop, so the highest designation rewards the ripest and sweetest wines (think of our tomato analogy!). Kabinett is the least ripe in this quality level, which gives it more of a green tomato vibe with some ripping acidity and a lighter body. Kabinetts can be either dry or sweet, so let's jump right to the good stuff.

Alc 8.0% Alc: Not all Rieslings are sweet, but this one is. How do I know that? Per our alcohol level chart in our Building Blocks section, this wine falls under 11% alcohol, so it's likely to be a sweet wine at 8%! I bet you knew that already so you get a gold star for that one. You're really nailing these math problems.

One more helpful German label tip: The word "trocken" means "dry" in German. Some labels just tell you in plain English... I mean German, which is extremely helpful.

ORANGE WINES

A category so old, it's now new again: orange wine. Orange wine was some of the first wine ever made by humanity in the Republic of Georgia. Orange wines are now a sensation sweeping the globe and generally get clumped in with "natural wines". Natural wines encompass the idea of making wines with "nothing added and nothing taken away", as wine critic Alice Feiring coined.

Gulp Hablo: The name of the producer.

Orange wine: Orange wines are also called "skin-contact wines". This is because orange wines are made with white wine grapes where the grape skins stay in contact with the juice, giving it a coppery/orange color and particular taste.

Imported by T Edwards Wines, LTD: This is the importer that brought the wine into the country.

Skin-fermented Verdejo 50% – Sauvignon Blanc 50%: The term "skin-fermented" is interchangeable with skin-contact or orange wine. Verdejo is a white wine grape regional to Spain.

How To Read A Wine Label

Parra Jimenez – Spain: This wine is made in Spain, if you weren't 100% sure.

Made with organic grapes certified organic by Sohiscert ES-ECO-002-CM: Some wineries practice organic methods, which means everything is organic except for paying the fee to have the "organic" logo on their label. Some producers feel that they don't have to have approval to be organic and use it almost as a F.U. to "the man", man.

1L: A notable anomaly from the 750ml we see for a typical bottle of wine!

A QUICK Q&A ABOUT ORANGE WINES:

Is orange wine made from oranges? No oranges here—it's white wine made like red wine. Imagine you're making white wine; you smoosh grapes in a bucket with all the seeds, stems, and skins, and let it sit. Well, that pigment and tannin seeps out into the juice, and tints the color a slight amber or orange color. The longer the skins sit with the juice, the darker the color will be. This also gives it a particular taste like bruised apples, dried apricots, and a bit of funk, which is something akin to sourdough or kombucha. I find that most orange wines have this flavor profile (except for a few examples) and our building block concepts are moot in this case.

Why are some orange wines cloudy? Back to our wine-in-a-bucket analogy—the wine will naturally have all of the bits of pieces of the grapes in there. Some winemakers decide to filter it to make it clear and some don't. It's a stylistic choice that can sometimes affect the funkiness of the wine. I find that that the cloudier it is the more polarizing it may be.

Will I like it? It can be a bit of an acquired taste, I say try it twice. Once to get over the initial shock of it, and a second time to see if you like it (or just drink rosé, that's cool too).

COMMON FAQS:

These are some common questions I get that might help you clarify some bits in your wine- purchasing journey.

HOW CAN I TELL IF A WINE IS SWEET:

When I ask people what kind of wines they like, 80% will tell me they like "something dry." I feel like Inigo Montoya from *The Princess Bride* and think, "You keep using that word. I don't think it means what you think it means."

You can keep the sugar in a wine and it will still taste dry.

Sugar is to wine like salt is to food. Salt isn't always used to add a salty quality to a dish but used as a flavor enhancer. Salt makes a steak taste steak-ier, a tabbouleh taste tabbouleh-ier, and even makes a chocolate chip cookie delightfully less sweet. It lifts and balances every component. If you had a Daiquiri with no sugar, and only lime juice and rum, you'd get a tart, bitter, boozy concoction you'd likely suck down purely to avoid embarrassment. The sugar sorta kinda makes it sweet, but its real job is to round out the whole drink, add a little body/richness, and make it more delicious. Every wine has some sugar in it, but that doesn't mean it's going to be a sweet wine. If you are curious about what a wine with zero sugar tastes like, you could look at a brut nature style of Champagne. I'd personally argue this beverage would be undrinkable if there were no bubbles to it.

Despite all the anti-sugar sentiment on the Internet, sugar in wine is your friend.

How To Read A Wine Label

Grape juice before fermentation is sweet, but the fermentation uses those sugars, and converts them to alcohol and carbon dioxide. Winemakers can stop fermentation early to maintain that natural sugar content. This is called residual sugar, and you may find that term on some more comprehensive labels. Otherwise, winemakers can add sugar at the end of the finished, fermented wine, and this is called chaptalization. I find that when people want something dry, these consumers might actually enjoy a wine with residual sugar but think the chaptalized wine is too sweet. You won't always be able to tell by looking at a label, but generally if a wine says "sweet wine" it has that candied, jammy, sweet flavor. Sometimes they won't tell you at all (I'm looking at you, California!). Shoutout to wineries: if you have a wine that has perceived sweetness, please include some clever marketing indication on the label.

If you're skittish about accidentally choosing a sweet wine, I'd recommend staying away from all New World or high-alcohol wines (over 15%). Even if they are technically dry, some people find the fruit-forward aspect of New World wines sugary sweet. Once you become more confident, move towards New World wines with an Old World influence. A Pinot Noir from the Willamette Valley in Oregon would be the best place to start on your journey into the balance of fruity and earthy. Only with enough tasting, especially if you get to taste wines side by side, will you start to understand what "sweet" really means to you.

How To Read A Wine Label

Then there are wines that are explicitly sweet, and you can tell by looking out for these key words on a wine label:

WINE SWEETNESS LEVELS

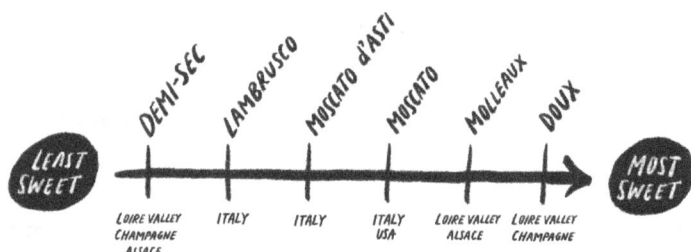

HOW TO PICK BETWEEN 5 SIMILAR WINES

Imagine this common scenario: you're at your local wine shop and you see five bottles of Bordeaux next to each other. How do you decide which one to buy?

I'm gonna make wine professionals mad. For all intents and purposes, all Bordeauxs are the same (I can hear the clanging of pitchforks from sommeliers and winemakers). Yes, there may be differences in the blend of grapes, what village it's from, or the quality levels, but the general idea is the same. When you're first starting out, just recognizing Bordeaux and knowing you want to buy a Bordeaux is a huge win. You have confirmed that you like Old World over New World, cooler-climate over warmer-climate flavors, and thick-skinned over thin-skinned grapes. You like something earthier, tarter, richer, and a bit of zip. If you can say that confidently, I have done my job.

Knowing the differences between Bordeauxs, now you've hit Level 2 of wine. You might know you like a Merlot-based blend over a Cabernet or you might know you prefer a winemaker who's a bit more hands off in the winemaking process. That's where the nerd shit comes in. That's when you start to buy the textbooks on your favorite region, and taste wines blind side by side to see if you can taste the subtle differences.

I see a lot of "Best of" lists. Whether it's for wine or for cheeseburgers, once you know you love something you can pick up the minutiae of what makes it special, unique, or mundane. Just like the cheeseburger critic might love a smashburger on a Martin's potato roll over a pub burger on house-made brioche, ultimately, your own personal preference will dictate how to choose between five different Bordeauxs, Napa Valley Cabernets, or Barolos. For example, I don't love many Napa Valley Cabernet Sauvignons, but I do love the more elegant, Old World style of Cathy Corison's Cabernet from Napa. Is it for everyone? Definitely not. But it's for me. Definitely yes. This is where you really sound like you know what you're talking about.

Ultimately, whether you're eating a cheeseburger or drinking a bottle of Bordeaux, even an okay one will still scratch the itch.

Quality-level specifications are created for the pursuit of excellence. Grand Crus, Premier Crus, and Classicos are great

How To Read A Wine Label

for people who have their feet wet. In my experience, most people who are buying wine at the grocery store aren't necessarily looking for excellence but for this-is- tasty-ness or nice-with-dinner-ness. With you in mind, dear reader, I am going to tell you to ignore the nuance of quality levels and just get the basics down.

In short, pick the cheapest to start with and go from there. If that's not a good enough answer for you, I'll let you in on a little secret that sommeliers use when they're deciding between two or five similar wines.

PERHAPS THE ONLY INFORMATION YOU NEED

Look at you go, cruising through labels like a pro, making informed decisions about your purchases. I'm real proud of ya. Getting the fundamentals down is great, but quickly you'll find labels with grapes and regions that we don't go over in this book. What do you do when you want to start exploring outside the lines?

I'll teach you a sommelier secret: the importer. The importer is essentially the middleman between the winemaker and the consumer. Each importer has their own taste and personality. So, instead of picking a favorite grape or region, you could pick a favorite importer! This can also be helpful if you're looking at five different Bordeauxs or Chardonnays, and you can just flip the bottle to check the back label and see if it's from an importer you like. I've included some of my favorites here. This is not an exhaustive list, but these are some of the key players with "personality" that I like to drink.

KOBRAND
FINE WINE AND SPIRITS
Since 1944

WINEBOW
FINE WINE + SPIRITS

**KERMIT LYNCH
WINE MERCHANT**

NOVOVINO
WINE CO.

VB
VINEYARD
BRANDS

ARTISTIC EPILOGUE

CAN I BE HONEST WITH YOU?

Despite me knowing all the knowledge in this book, I too will buy a wine simply because I like the label. So, if you skimmed this book and thought, "I just love the art and fonts," I made this section for you. These are a few of my favorite labels, along with the artist's inspiration (if they're still alive!). After all, there is usually an artist hired to create the art on the label and they don't always have a chance to represent themselves. Take these last few pages just to soak it all in—who knows, maybe you'll be inspired to make your own label at the end!

Catena Zapata 'Argentino' Malbec 2019

Nicolas Catena, founder of Catena Zapata, says: "Designed by Stranger & Stranger, with the artwork supplied by Rick Shaefer, the label depicts four female figures which embody different milestones in the history of Argentina's treasured grape variety.

The epic tale of the noble Malbec grape is like no other, and the label for Catena Zapata Malbec Argentino pays tribute to the variety's history in France and its rise in Argentina. Four female figures embody different landmarks in the history of the grape. Eleanor of Aquitaine represents the birth of Malbec. She is a strong, Old World presence, lingering at the bridge in Cahors, where Malbec came into its own. Next, the immigrant symbolizes the movement to the New World, and the unknown explorers and adventurers who connected Europe with the Americas. Phylloxera personifies the death of Malbec in the Old World, which enabled its

How To Read A Wine Label

rebirth in the New. Finally, there is Bodega Catena Zapata, represented by Adrianna Catena, who depicts birth, earth, and motherhood, sharing the riches of the New World. Today, the Catena family's fourth generation leads the high-altitude renaissance in Argentina. We are returning Malbec to the sky... where it belongs."

Johan Vineyards 'Drueskall' Pinot Gris 2022

Morgan Beck, winemaker at Johan Vineyards, says: "We actually found [our artist Yong Hong] Zhong on Instagram of all places! We love his work, and once I met him. I realized we really connected on the desire to capture an artistic expression of a place—he does this through painting, and we do this in the crafting of a wine. It's been an incredible experience working with him... I start by creating a mood board and writing down my goals and 'feelings' that go into crafting a wine, what I look for when blending the wine, and what the desired experience is for the consumer when they work through a bottle of the wine. I taste in colors, so I often have an idea of the color palette I'm hoping for, and some ideas of a specific phenomenon or event that happens on the property that invokes the same feelings that I feel when making/ tasting the wine. It's a really fun and unique process working through the creation of a label with him... I never thought it would be as fulfilling as it is!"

How To Read A Wine Label

Clos Cibonne Cotes de Provence Rose Tradition 2023

This was the first label that I was drawn to when working in a Michelin-star restaurant. The same restaurant is where I received the advice and unofficial motto of this book, which is, "learn every single word on the label". Something about its illustrative nature, the sepia tones, and the style of the buildings commands a sense of place. I can nearly smell the heat radiating off the stone house. Its biggest word, 'Tibouren', was a mystery to me at the time. A healthy reminder that not long ago, I was much like you, dear reader, and didn't know if Tibouren was a grape, region, or the name of the wine (Bonus points if you know!). It was also my first foray into Provence wine that was not pink lemonade-y rosé, but something deeply complex and even age-able. This family-run winery has a long lineage of winemaking and takes on the Old World ethos of tradition into the labels themselves, which haven't changed in the past 100 years. This is the label that piqued my curiosity for wine at the beginning of my career, and I hope that this book will ignite that same curiosity in you.

How To Read A Wine Label

CREATE YOUR OWN LABEL!

A label can take many creative directions: it can be a homage to the past and the history of the winery or it can just be a pure personal expression.. If you were to make a label, what would it look like? I'll start:

My beautiful wine label, found in a coloring book from my in-laws place in Wisconsin. This was either drawn by a 9-year-old or my 42-year-old sister-in-law, but we'll never know. I know for a fact that there are wine labels that take inspiration from their kids for artwork, so that's nothing new. I have no strong family ties to traditional winemaking or feel a need to follow the rules of an Old World label. I'm here to have a nice time and drink something fun with friends. Horsin' Around is a testament to that.

Horsin' Around: The cuvée, or the name of the wine. We're just having a good time here.

Domaine Slik: The name of the producer. Although this wine is going to be made in the USA, I use the word 'Domaine' cause I think it sounds fancier and fits the vibe of the horse a bit more. Slik is the tail end of my last anime CheSLIK and is also the name of my already existing S-Corp so let's just make our lives easier shall we?

Lake Michigan Shore AVA: The location of the winery in Michigan. AVA stands for American Viticultural Region and is one of the 5 AVAs in Michigan. With the global climate getting warmer, Michigan is in prime real estate to create amazing wine. I'm starting a winery here ot get ahead of the curve (if someone wants to be an investor, just give me a call). This cool-climate, New World region may remind you of the Willamette Valley in Oregon in the near future.

Pinot Noir: The name of the grape. My favorite red wines are usually light-bodied and have a bit of chill on them. Pinot Noir makes me happy.

2024: The vintage. I'm looking for a fresh, young wine with a free spirit. Much like the horse on the label.

YOUR TURN!

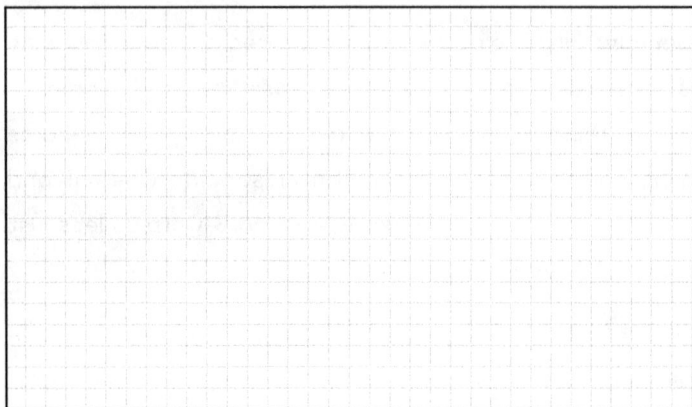

PRODUCER

_____

_____

_____

NAME OF WINE

_____

_____

_____

GRAPE

_____

_____

_____

VINTAGE

_____

_____

PLACE

_____

_____

STORY

_____

_____

WHAT DOES IT TASTE LIKE?

_____

_____

_____

_____

_____

_____

_____

www.ingramcontent.com/pod-product-compliance
Lightning Source LLC
Chambersburg PA
CBHW070756300326
41914CB00053B/688